Pot Likker

Stories for
Teachers and Learners

Larry Grant Coleman and
Deborah Peaks Coleman
editors

The Pilgrim Press
Cleveland, Ohio

The Pilgrim Press, 700 Prospect Avenue, Cleveland, Ohio 44115-1100
www.pilgrimpress.com

Printed in the United States of America on acid-free paper

06   05   04   03   02   01   5   4   3   2   1

Library of Congress Cataloging-in-Publication Data
Pot likker : stories for teachers and learners / Larry Grant Coleman and Deborah Peaks
Coleman, eds.
    p.   cm.
    Includes bibliographical references.
    ISBN 0-8298-1409-4 (paper)
    1. Education—Anecdotes.   2. Teaching—Anecdotes.   3. Learning—Anecdotes.   I. Coleman, Larry Grant, 1946- II. Coleman, Deborah Peaks, 1957- III. Title.

LA23 .P59   2001
370—dc21

                                                      2001024586

Contents

Preface

WE CONTINUE TO BELIEVE that storytelling is the most powerful means of communicating and teaching us about people, concepts, events, objects, and experiences. This volume of stories, *Pot Likker Stories for Teachers and Learners*, is designed to entertain and inspire readers. It also intends to provide teachers, leaders, parents, and others with valuable ideas and techniques for creating success, for inspiring positive change, and for fostering growth in the people whose lives they touch. We have included personal experience stories and folktales from persons throughout the country. These stories speak to achievement, transformation, perseverance, and expectations.

The phrase *pot likker*, often used by contemporary restaurant chefs, originated in the folk traditions of African captives during the early days of slavery in America. Its use has continued over generations, particularly in the American south and among African Americans. The highly nutritious broth left over from cooking vegetables like collard greens, mustard greens, cabbage, or turnip greens (occasionally seasoned with spices and differerent kinds of meat) was branded as pot likker. It was thought to have healing powers and was often stored and given as food or as a medicinal potion to sick persons.

Realizing that in the minds of many pot likker symbolizes nourishment for the human body, *Pot Likker Stories for Teachers and*

Learners aims to nourish one's mind, heart, and soul. These are tales from a diverse collection of authors of various cultural, ethnic, and racial backgrounds. They are stories that teach in more ways than one. In the more conventional sense, the narratives collected here touch the field of education and the experiences of teachers and learners in learning environments: elementary, middle, and high school or college. They show people struggling to overcome academic failure or personal and cultural obstacles to their development. They also illustrate techniques that teachers and learners have used to propel themselves forward.

These tales demonstrate that teachers, mentors, coaches, and leaders who are in charge of helping others achieve are able to impact learners and followers in productive or nonproductive ways. Consequently, those teachers have a great responsibility to the learner. Psychologist Haim Ginott, author of *Teacher and Child*, remembers the time as a young teacher when he considered the following idea: "I've come to the frightening conclusion, I am the decisive element in the classroom. It is my personal approach that creates the climate. It is my daily mood that makes the weather. . . . As a teacher I possess tremendous power to make a child's life miserable or joyous."

In a different way, these anecdotes are stories that teach because several of them teach lessons about life and human behavior. They include a moral point. They provide us insight on how to be alert and responsible so that we do not miss obvious chances for achievement and growth.

The first section of this book, "Transformation," includes stories about people who have been in learning situations where they have had to endure deep emotional challenges and difficulties. They more than endured the difficulties, they triumphed. These people experienced breakthroughs and transformations in their development because of the caring, supportive teachers, parents, mentors, and friends in their lives.

Like the statement from Dr. Ginott, the second section, "The Impact of Expectations," demonstrates the power of leaders, counselors, and teachers to "control the weather" in a learner's life. The expectations they set can have positive or negative effects. In most of these tales, the teacher had strong, positive expectations that yielded great results in the lives of the learners.

The section on "Unique Achievement" demonstrates the power of individual persons to be resilient and bring their own unique capabilities to bear on challenging learning situations. The "Perseverance" section contains stories that emphasize the value of moving beyond mediocrity to seek and achieve a high standard. The stories demonstrate that, given the right support and the appropriate level of challenge, individual persons can accomplish more than they thought they could, even in the face of overwhelming obstacles.

The final section is called "The Storyteller's Circle" because the writers in this section have developed a fascination for the storytelling process and have incorporated that process into both original tales and variants of folktales. These writers also share with readers a little about the power and effectiveness of storytelling to energize teaching and learning situations.

We hope that you enjoy, use, tell, and retell the stories that are in this collection.

Larry Grant Coleman and
Deborah Peaks Coleman, editors

PART ONE

Transformation

Change your mind and you will change your life.
— TRADITIONAL AMERICAN PROVERB

THESE STORIES CAPTURE the occurrence of powerful change in people's lives. These are not just any kind of changes; they are life-saving changes that ultimately will have an impact on the lives of thousands of the people who will come into contact with the teachers and leaders depicted in the stories.

꿰꿰꿰 1 꿰꿰꿰

It Is Never Too Late

Linda Vilches

EVER SINCE THE FIRST DAY of kindergarten, I knew what I wanted to be when I grew up. I wanted to be a teacher just like Mrs. Braverman. All through elementary school I listened to every word my teachers said; after all, they were my role models. I studied hard and always made the honor roll. At eighth grade graduation, I even received the Principal's Award.

In high school, I felt that I was on my way. My freshman year schedule was that of a college-bound student. At the end of my first year in high school, my parents and I met with my guidance counselor to discuss a course of study for the following year. My guidance counselor asked me what I intended to study in college. I explained that I wanted to become a teacher. I couldn't believe what happened next. The guidance counselor told my parents that this was unacceptable. Didn't I know that there was an abundance of teachers and that I would never get a job? Not only that, how were my parents going to come up with the money for college? In a matter of a few moments, my life-long dream was destroyed.

It was then decided that I should enroll in one of the B.O.C.E.S. (Board of Cooperative Educational Services) courses. Wouldn't I like to be a hairdresser? Well, needless to say, that is exactly what happened. From my sophomore year through my senior year, I attended the cosmetology classes for half the day and then returned to school to take the required courses needed for graduating with a regent's diploma. But my heart wasn't in it. After the first year, I wanted to drop cosmetology. I didn't like it and couldn't see myself working in this field. My counselor wouldn't let me drop the class without my parents' consent, and my parents wouldn't sign the paper. When nobody would listen to me when I told them what I really wanted, I started not to care. There were many times that I missed the bus "accidentally on purpose." I almost didn't graduate because I never went to gym class. Did I care? Not at all.

After graduating by the skin of my teeth, I started working full time in a beauty parlor. Still, my heart was not in it. I didn't even last a year as a hairdresser. From the time I graduated high school until I was 27 years old, I bounced from job to job. Work was okay, but never fulfilling. At that time, I had been married for seven years and had a four-year-old daughter.

One day the ESL (English as a Second Language) teacher from the school where my mother worked as an office aide called and asked if I would be interested in working as his aide because I knew a little Spanish. I took the job thinking that with my daughter starting kindergarten the following year, my work schedule would be the same as her school schedule.

Within the first week on the job, I was asked to substitute teach for the fifth grade class. I walked up to the room not expecting too much; after all, what students listen to a sub? During the first lesson, something magical happened. The class and I seemed to connect. They were asking questions, and I saw the spark of understanding in some of their eyes. I was hooked. Wasn't this what I originally wanted to do?

The ESL teacher talked to me about going to college. He said it was never too late and that I should seriously think about it. All of a sudden, the old feelings of wanting to be a teacher became so strong that it was all I could think about. With the support of my husband, I enrolled in two college classes over the summer. I wanted to get the feel of going back to school to see if I could handle it. That fall, I enrolled in college full time. I worked full-time at the school and then attended college classes during the late afternoon and evenings. When I came home, I usually stayed up until 2:00 a.m. doing all the required reading and studying. Every time I thought about stopping the crazy schedule I had, I would remember the magic I felt in the classroom and studied harder. I graduated suma cum laude with a 3.975 GPA. Not bad for a person who was told to forget about their dream.

꧁ 2 ꧂

To Be Seen Is to Be Known

ELEANOR HOOKS

As I DRIVE ALONG A WINDING country road, I reflect on a simple human experience—being really seen. How often do we see another person, I mean, really see him? So often what we think we are seeing is not the person at all, but mere images—drama written and enacted for our benefit, for our reaction. As the road finally rolls to the entrance to my neighborhood, I am suddenly pulled back in time, nearly twenty years ago, when a teenage boy allowed me to see him.

I was working in a typical 1980s high school as a guidance counselor. I loved the students, at least, most of them. Even some of the challenging ones were endearing in an odd sort of way. One day, a particular challenge got the best of me.

Philip had the habit of wearing all black clothing accessorized with spike bracelets and anklets. He wore numerous neck chains that hung in a menacing tangle around his neck. He almost always wore tee shirts with pictures of dragons or snakes spitting fire or coiled to strike. A worn black leather biker's jacket was his constant companion, even on warm spring or fall days.

Yes, Philip was quite a sight. But that's not the whole story. He was suspected of being the leader of a gang, and although no adult ever witnessed a drug deal, he was suspected of dealing drugs as well. He rarely attended class. Instead, he hung out in the halls, sometimes disappearing into the bathrooms where he was often smoked out by male teachers.

As Philip's counselor, I had tried to encourage him to be more a student and less a threat to himself and others. We talked. I listened. He promised. He did not change. But one day, my frustration with him was at its peak.

I approached Philip as he lingered in the hallway. "Philip, come with me to my office. I want to talk to you," I said, prepared to talk, listen, and hear empty promises. Instead, I took a long look at Philip as he reluctantly sprawled himself into a chair in my office. I had positioned myself in a chair a few feet away, but bravely not behind the desk. After looking at him for a few moments, I said, "Philip, I'm really scared of you." A smug look flickered briefly across his face, then a broad smile grew handsomely in its place.

Philip never smiled. I sensed that something was different so I continued, "Your clothes make me scared. What makes you decide to dress so differently from the other students?" Philip searched me with his eyes for signs of sincerity. "Well, Ms. Edwards, there's something about me you probably don't know. My dad is Phillipino. I know I don't look Phillipino, but I am. My mom's an American, but my dad's from the Philippines."

Probably noticing that I wasn't repulsed by this revelation, he continued, "When I came to the United States, I was six years old. My dad wanted me to be proud of him being a Philippino, so he made me wear traditional Philippino clothes. I cried every morning because he made me wear 'em." A look of pain and shame now covered the face that had a handsome smile only minutes earlier. Philip continued his story, "My father didn't care that the kids made fun of me and beat me up every day, because they said I wore funny clothes." "But," he continued, "I couldn't take it any more by the time I was eleven." I thought to myself, "what an awful thing to endure."

Philip, determined to help me to see him, continued, "One day I told my father I was not going to wear those clothes any more. My mom and dad got into a fight about it, but I won!" He nodded his head triumphantly, like a prizefighter who had just knocked down an opponent. "From that day, I decided that kids were gonna be afraid of me. I wasn't gonna let anybody else beat me up anymore!" Smiling again he said, "That's when I decided to dress tough. Nobody bothers me now." Finally, I was able to really see Philip—the person that he was, not just his image.

I decided to seize the power of the moment to fulfill my own goal: Find a way to make it okay for Philip to be a student, not a menace. I told him that I appreciated his sharing such a tough and personal story with me. I then told him that I believed that he knew the power of influence. He had used his influence in a destructive way sometimes, though. He nodded, probably expecting a lecture.

Instead, we talked about leadership abilities and how leaders can influence others to do positive things. I shared with him my frustration with students who hang out in the halls instead of going to class. I let him know that I had expectations that all my students could be successful, but that it required some sacrifice, some endurance. I mentioned that it took some fortitude for him to go to school when he was six. He seemed to understand that I was asking for his help, his leadership. I entreated, "Philip, would you help me to clear the halls and encourage the students to go to class? Would you tell them that they need to have endurance in order to achieve?" I thought he'd think I was being a little melodramatic, but I believed that he understood my meaning. During the next few weeks, the halls cleared. Philip went to class. And I focused my energies on other challenges, knowing that I had a new ally.

Matthias

Rev. Cyril G. Guerra Jr.

HE PAUSED AND THOUGHT about cutting class, but Mr. McMahon had already seen him in the cafeteria. So he continued up two flights of stairs to his English class. Today Mr. McMahon would grade them in declamation. Declamation was simply standing in front of the class and reciting a speech or poem. Matthias had not memorized anything, but he had already devised a plan and hoped it would work. He walked into Mr. McMahon's room and swaggered to his seat in the back. He turned to his friend Kevin and said "Wassup" before taking his seat.

Kevin asked, "You ready for declamation?"

Matthias answered, "Yeah."

Kevin looked surprised. "What you gonna do?"

"I'ma say a song."

Kevin looked even more surprised and intrigued. "A song?"

"Yeah, I'ma say "Goodbye Love" by Guy."

Kevin laughed and placed his hand over his mouth. "Man, you know you can't get up there and recite a song."

Matthias looked at him and smiled, "You know it's a song . . . and I know it's a song, but he don't know that. I'ma just say that it's a poem from an African American poetry book. He'll never know the difference."

One by one Mr. McMahon called students up to the front to deliver their speeches or poems. Some of the students delivered them with passion. Others had undoubtedly learned their pieces but delivered them in monotone, almost putting classmates to sleep. And still others stumbled and fumbled to remember their lines. Finally, it was Matthias's turn. He stood up and confidently walked to the front of the room. He began speak-

ing with authority: "The name of my poem is" Goodbye Love"
by Theodore Riles." Matthias thought that Theodore Riles
sounded much more poetic than Teddy Riley, the hip-hop artist
who was truly responsible for this popular R & B hit.

Matthias took a deep breath and began to recite: "Even
though I hate to leave, for I cried as I walked out the door./
Temptation is asking me to stay, but we've been through the
same trials and tribulations before." Matthias walked from side
to side as he eloquently delivered a flawless presentation that
would have made Langston Hughes proud. He was mindful of
making minor changes to the song so that it would not include
any "ooh baby's" or "ooh girl's." Upon finishing, the class gave
him rousing applause.

As Matthias returned to his seat, Kevin smiled and said, "Boy,
you know you crazy, right?" Fortunately, Mr. McMahon suspected
no foul play, and gave Matthias an A in declamation.

Matthias's cunning had earned him a minor victory and eased
his anxiety for a short time. Unfortunately, the feelings of loneli-
ness and inadequacy began to build once again. Though he had
managed to fool Mr. McMahon, he couldn't fool himself. He
was once again trying to get over. The seventh period bell rang,
and the students rushed out of the class. Matthias slowly rose
and began the long trek back to his homeroom. When he had
finally arrived, Ms. Jackson was already distributing report cards.
The moment of truth was here, but Matthias already knew what
to expect. This was his second time in the tenth grade, and he
was still failing every class except PE. He had always performed
well in school up until his father's untimely death from cancer.
Since his freshman year, there was a slow, but obvious, academic
slide. Matthias outwardly refused to attribute his low grades to
his father's death, yet deep down inside he was still trying to
cope with the loss. There were so many emotions swirling around
in him. He felt guilty for letting his family down. He felt stupid
as he watched his friends move up, while he remained stagnant.

His stomach turned as he thought about having to listen to all of his relatives' lectures. Finally, there was the frustration from knowing that he could perform better than this. Ms. Jackson gave Matthias his report card. He folded the paper and stuck it in his Eastpak without even looking at it. He left the room and made a quick stop at his locker to drop off some books. Then he rushed to catch the #22 bus. On the way he saw Kevin. "Yo Matt. We goin' to Boston House of Pizza, you wanna roll?"

"Naw, I got some things to take care of."

"Alright man, I'll see you tomorrow."

"Yeah, later."

Although it was late April, the air was still quite chilly. As he waited for the bus, Matthias said a brief and silent prayer, "Lord, I'm tired of failing, and I'm tired of struggling. Please help me to do the right thing. Amen." The #22 arrived in just under two minutes. Matthias stepped up into the bus and showed the driver his student MBTA pass. He walked to the rear of the bus and was surprised to see one of his old running buddies, Isaiah. Isaiah was two years older than Matthias. He had attended Metropolitan but transferred to another school. Ironically, Isaiah had been in a similar situation as Matthias. He had also been retained in the tenth grade, before transferring.

"Wassup, Isaiah?"

Isaiah smiled, happy to see his little partner in crime. "Wassup, Matt?"

The two boys shook hands and Matthias asked, "What school you at now?"

"Joseph Smith."

"How you like it over there?"

Isaiah leaned back in his seat and said, "Man, to be honest. Leaving Metropolitan was the best thing I could have done."

"Why you say that?" was Matthias' response.

Isaiah began, "When I was there, everybody and their momma was tellin' me I needed an education, but dat wasn't on my mind at the time. I finally realized that I didn't do my work because I didn't want the education. Everybody else wanted it for me. I looked around and noticed that most of the brothers from around the way were on hard times. The ones I looked up to were still robbin' folks. I didn't want that, and I realized that bein' stupid ain't cool. I decided that I wanted the education for myself. Can't get nowhere without it. Then, when I was tryin' to get it together, nobody at Metro wanted to gimme a chance. So, I had to leave, or get kept back again. I had to get out of that situation, so I could start all over again. A new place, a new mindset."

Matthias listened intently. Isaiah stood up and said "Yo, this is my stop, keep your head up."

Matthias replied, "Awright man," as they shook hands again. The bus rolled to a stop, and Isaiah stepped off. As the doors closed and the bus rolled on, Matthias thought about the conversation.

It dawned on him that because of his past performance, all of the teachers expected him to fail. This enraged him. He thought, "They're expecting me to fail, and I'm playin' the game along with them. I refuse to fail!" The more he thought, the more he realized that he had to prove all of them wrong, no matter how hard the work. He had gained some invaluable insight from this five-minute conversation. He realized that it was never too late to turn things around and that he had to thirst for success before it would come. Matthias looked up to the sky feeling that he had gotten the answer he was looking for. Slowly and silently he mouthed, "Thank You."

Two years later, Matthias sat in the large auditorium at Joseph Smith High School. He listened as James Jones, the principal, spoke at the commencement of the class of 1991. Mr. Jones smiled and offered congratulations to the graduating class. After delivering the usual commencement speech, Mr. Jones said, "And now I'd like to introduce the class of 1991's senior class president!" Everyone stood up and gave a long standing ovation. Matthias stood up, walked to the podium, smiled, looked upwards, and again silently mouthed, "Thank You."

"Reyes" of Brilliance

EDWARD R. ROBINSON

IN MY TENTH GRADE South Bronx's high school math class, I had a student named Reyes Aviles. Reyes's junior high school's record indicated that he was a "hyperactive, low-achieving . . . distracting influence in the classroom." The school's guidance counselor advised me: "If I were you, I'd give him some easy, busy work to keep him occupied." But, as was my custom, I did not listen to the negative words of the guidance counselor; nor did I pay any attention to any of the unflattering comments that were written on his junior high school's record. To the contrary, I gave Reyes class work that was much more demanding than what was required in the course curriculum. For example, I had Reyes "derive" proofs for all of the theorems that we used in the classroom lessons. And you know what? Reyes always handed in flawless proofs to these assigned theorems.

And Reyes' exceptional abilities in the classroom were not just limited to solving rigorous math proofs either. His classroom behavior (in direct opposition to what was indicated on his junior high school's record) was truly exemplary. He was always punctual, attentive to the lessons, and he followed all classroom rules. For example, when answering a question in the class, he would always raise his hand and be recognized by me before talking aloud.

Further, Reyes was one of the most selfless students that I had ever taught. Anytime one of his fellow students had difficulty understanding the work in the class, he would always be the first person to offer his time and talent to help the student. Oftentimes, his services to a student would go far beyond classroom hours.

By the end of the first week of having Reyes in the class, I started singing his praises throughout the school, advising all of his subject teachers that if they wanted to get the best out of him, they should give him challenging work. I would tell each of his teachers: "Don't believe what you read in his junior high school's record because it does not accurately reflects his true abilities and character."

Apparently, Reyes's subject teachers had heeded my advice to them because at the end of the school term Reyes would become the number-one-academically-ranked student in the entire tenth grade class (450 students—which included college bound and honors students). I, again, went around the school and sang his praises.

Over the next two years, as the school's college advisor, I (despite receiving opposition from some of the school's officials) was able to help Reyes gain enrollment in area colleges' enrichment programs. The college administrators of these programs would call or write me on numerous occasions to tell me of Reyes's "outstanding work ethic and unwavering desire to achieve excellence in all assigned tasks."

To no one's surprise, Reyes would become the valedictorian of his senior class. Midway through delivering the valedictorian speech, he paused and turned in my direction. "Thank you, Mr. Robinson," he said. "Thank you for helping me realize my potential. Your belief in my abilities as a good math student helped to bring the best out of me. Your belief in me as a good person enabled others to see the best in me."

And at his high school graduation—to my great delight—Reyes would be awarded the gold medal for "highest academic achievement in mathematics." It would also be announced at the graduation that Reyes would receive a four-year scholarship to Harvard University.

Four years following his graduation from high school, Reyes would graduate Magna Cum Laude from Harvard University. At present, Reyes is in his third year (on full scholarship) at Harvard University Medical School. Becoming a medical doctor has always been Reyes's dream. You see, as a high school student, he used to spend a lot of his time in local Medicaid clinics with his mother, who suffers from chronic asthma. He used to marvel at the healing power of the doctors, but didn't like the way some of them treated his mother. Reyes said, "I will open my own clinic someday."

ᚎᚎᚎ **5** ᚎᚎᚎ

Thank You, Joey

DIANE FERLATTE

I AM A PROFESSIONAL STORYTELLER who never thought I would be a storyteller in a million years. You never know how your life is going to change. One day my life was going one way and the next day it was going another. My last day job was as an office worker, working for the International Longshoreman's Warehouse Union in San Francisco. I worked there for seventeen years on the same job, and never even thought about storytelling. Funny thing is, I grew up hearing stories. I was steeped in stories. I spent a lot of time on my grandparent's porch in Louisiana listening to stories. I heard stories of family and history, folk tales, joke tales, ghost tales, sometimes even tall tales, and of course Bible stories. Growing up in the South you could go from porch to porch and hear some kind of story. But as a kid I didn't realize how important stories were or how important they would become in my life.

My grandfather lived to be 107 years old and he knew and told many stories. But do you think I remember many of his stories? NO! I was just a kid and wasn't even paying attention half the time. Now he's gone and I wish I had taken the time to listen a little more carefully. My father, who was the main storyteller in my life whom we called Popi, was Mister Funny. He would tell you a story even if you didn't want to hear one. And my mother's story—what a story! The day she was born was the day her mother died. The stories of her life that she passed on to me continue to give me strength and faith to this very day. She always said, tough times come but they don't last, tough people do. Stories were always such a natural part of my life, but I didn't have a clue how important they were until I adopted my children.

My husband and I adopted a little girl first. She was six weeks old and slept all night. Everything was wonderful—until we adopted a boy. We drove all the way from Oakland to Los Angeles to get him. My daughter asked, "When am I going to see my new brother?" I said, "It won't be long."

When we got to Los Angeles, they put us in a room to wait. Finally they brought Joey in. He was three-and-a-half-years old, and he was so cute. When he first saw us, do you know what he said? Do you think he said "Mama?" No. "Daddy?" No. He screamed, "Ahhhhh, I want my other mother!" I felt so sorry for this little boy. He didn't know us, and he was scared to death. So he started crying. We didn't know what to do. We started crying. My daughter, Cicely, then two-and-a-half, looked up at him and said, "Don't cry, don't cry, don't cry, boy." She took his hand, and he stopped crying. What a relief, but when we got him home things got worse. At three-and-a-half, this boy came with stories.

One story was that the foster mother who had him last had six other children and put them all in front of the TV all day. So you know that when he came to our house, we had a big problem. I tried to be a good mother. I got a nice little bedtime story to read to my daughter and new son. My daughter looked forward to it and would say, "Read the story, Mama, read the story." I said, "Okay baby, sit down." When I started to read the story, my new son whined, "I want to watch TV." I said, "No, honey, we're having a bedtime story, okay?" "No! I want to watch TV." I thought to myself, "What kind of kid is this?" I kept trying to read the book, but he had no attention span at all. Finally I realized that I was reading to a TV brain. How do you get a TV brain to listen?

The book I was reading, I dumped that book, and got a new book with a few more interesting characters in it. This book just happened to have a witch in it . . . eeeh! eh! eh! Boy did he jump, and I'm sure he thought, "Maybe I better listen." If there was a dog in the story, you know what I did . . . grrrr, ruuuuf, ruuuf! If there was a cat . . . meow. And if there was an old woman, I became that old woman. I did everything to get him to listen. I changed the way I was reading. I read the story like I was telling it. That old tradition I had grown up with was coming back to me. I became the characters, I used pauses, sound effects, body language, and I noticed that he was listening like it was live TV. One night he said to me, "Mama, are we going to have the bedtime story tonight?" I thought, "Ha, ha, I've got him now."

Every week we would all go to the library and get new books with more interesting characters. On Saturday mornings, we would go to the cultural center in Berkeley for the children's shows. We would see storytellers, singers, dancers, puppet shows, and children's theater. No matter what we did, he still would want to watch TV, and he would if I let him. I didn't let him. In preparing him to go to pre-school with his sister, I began not only reading but introducing him to the sounds that made up the words and the alphabet, which he knew nothing about even though he was now four years old. Trying to teach him his colors, numbers, and alphabet was not easy. My daughter, who already knew her ABCs, was counting, knew some phonics, and even would pick up a book and pretend to read with the same expression in her voice that she heard in mine. Joey liked listening to the stories and singing a few songs, but was not at all interested in learning the ABCs.

One night we had a sleepover with my kids and two other kids. One of the kids, who was seven, asked if he could read the story that night. I said sure. I read a few lines and Damon read a few lines. I noticed that Joey had a look of shock on his face seeing a kid read. Later on that night he asked me, "How did Damon know how to read?" I told him that Damon knows his sounds. Once you learn the sounds you can read. And it seemed to me at that moment I saw a new Joey. He wanted to read just like Damon. So I went out and bought a blackboard and some chalk and we started working on sounds from A to Z. Before too long, he was sounding out words and trying to read. I would read a line, Cicely would read a line, and Joey would read a line. Sometimes when the story got good, he would try to read my lines. By the time he was in the first grade, he was not only reading, but reading with expression as if he were telling the story. In the second grade he won first place in the Oakland School District Martin Luther King Jr. Oratorical Contest.

I'm happy to say that all through school Joey was an avid reader. He would read to pass the time when TV was forbidden because he was on punishment, which was a lot of the time— but that's another story. He's still reading today as he goes to college.

My story comes full circle when I realize that in trying to lay the foundation for Joey to do well and succeed in school, I found myself returning to my foundations. Using the oral tradition I was familiar with as a kid, I incorporated that background into trying to teach Joey to pay attention, to concentrate, and then to read. Shortly thereafter, I was asked to tell some stories at a Christmas church function for underprivileged kids. Church members and guests heard me there, asked me to tell stories at other functions, and, lo and behold, a career was born. More and more requests to tell stories kept coming in so that I took a chance and left my job of seventeen years to tell stories full time. Happily, I have never looked back. I have traveled the country and the world telling stories as a professional storyteller since that time and have loved every minute of it. Thank you, Joey.

꿰꿰꿰 6 꿰꿰꿰

The Long Journey to Success

Mimi Leibman

He was small for his age, he was our baby, and he did not like going to school. So when we received the news at the end of kindergarten that Matthew had a learning disability, we were alarmed. However, we put his fate into the hands of the experts and he appeared to be well suited for the multi-sensory first grade class he attended the following year.

In second grade, Matt decided that he was dumb because they were giving him first grade material to read. They had not bothered to camouflage the material, and he was smart enough to get that message. At our request, a private psychologist tested him and advised us to remove him from the learning disabilities program because it was doing him more harm than good, causing him to doubt himself. With great trepidation we followed his advice even though we were warned by the school personnel that he would never succeed if he did not get the special help they were offering.

This began a long journey for our family. We consulted many experts along the way who supported Matt's insistence that he attend regular classes. This sometimes troubled us, but we respected his decision. While his learning problem was mild enough for him to compensate with lots of support from the family, there were clearly costs to him as well. He had to work harder and longer and it frustrated him that it seemed to come so much easier to many of his friends.

The message we gave to Matthew at home was consistent. We told him that he was very smart, but that he learned differently from others so that it took longer for him to finish his work. However, the messages he received at school were not always as encouraging, and he continued to doubt his ability to succeed. School was always a chore for him, but he was determined to conquer it. As the years went on, he gained greater confidence and began to believe that he could succeed if he worked hard. The only special help he received over those years was to take college entrance exams under untimed conditions.

In his freshman year of college, he called home in a panic. How was he ever going to read all of the material they assigned? We reminded him that it would just take him longer to accomplish and that he might not be able to party as often as his fellow students did, but that he could do it. We also suggested that he avail himself of the special services the college offered, but he once again stubbornly refused.

Matthew decided early on that he wanted to become a doctor. Knowing the amount of schooling and competition that this entailed concerned us, but he was determined that he could accomplish whatever he set his sights on. When he began the application and interview process for medical school, we asked him how he might feel at a highly competitive school with fellow students from all of the top colleges in the country. His words were music to our ears. He said that he had learned that if he worked hard at something, he could accomplish anything he wanted. And he has proven to himself and to us that he is absolutely correct.

Last year, when Matthew received exemplary scores on his medical boards and was accepted into his first choice of residency programs in orthopedic surgery, he told us that he finally felt smart for the first time in his life. It was a long and arduous journey for him and our family, but he had finally achieved what we had hoped for him all of his life. When he took his Hippocratic Oath at his medical school graduation, his older sister cried as she said, "I can't believe that this accomplished young man is the same person as that scared little boy in kindergarten!"

<h1 align="center">毛毛毛 7 毛毛毛</h1>

You Are Going to Pass

JOSEPH PETRELLA

I WAS BORN IN 1932 to Italian immigrants parents in the Fordham section of the Bronx, an Italian neighborhood in New York City also known as Little Italy. Neither one of my parents advanced past the sixth grade, and education was never a priority in my family. I was the fourth son and the only one of the four to complete high school. I did not learn to speak English until I went to public school.

After completing elementary and junior high school programs, I attended Theodore Roosevelt High School in the Bronx, where I managed to graduate with an academic diploma. My parents expected me to quit school and go to work. I could not continue to live with them without contributing to family expenses. My high school teachers encouraged me to go to college, and I was eligible to attend City College of New York (CCNY), which was tuition-free at that time. In order to go to college and live at home, I had to work a full-time job and attend college classes in late afternoons and evenings. Mine was not a "Father Knows Best" type of family—you either contributed or were shown the door. Unfortunately, two of my brothers got into trouble with the law and one was actually incarcerated for several years.

It was the public schools that had encouraged me to continue with my education, and it was the free tuition program at City College that allowed me to improve my life and create a brighter future for myself.

While I was at Theodore Roosevelt High School, I took Intermediate Algebra in my senior year. Unfortunately, in mid-semester, our mathematics teacher suddenly died and the class was subjected to a series of substitute teachers for several weeks. Somehow, I managed to achieve a 65% on the Regents Exam, and the mathematics chairman decided to give me a passing grade for the semester so I could graduate on time. This turned out to be a poor decision because I was not able to overcome a serious deficiency in prerequisite knowledge of mathematics when I attended City College of New York.

In September, 1949, I registered for my freshman year at CCNY and, because I was working days, I had to take late afternoon and evening courses. One of the required courses was Math 61, and the only time I could fit it in was 4:00 p.m. Because of my lack of instruction during my final year of mathematics at Roosevelt High School, I found the course to be extremely difficult. The instructor, Professor K, was very unsympathetic and uncaring. I failed the course. For the next two years I dropped the course three times and failed it once more. In each case, Professor K was the only instructor to offer the class at a time I could fit in.

I was in my senior year and still had not passed the required Math 61—it had become a mental block for me, and I just couldn't get through the course. With only eleven credits needed for my B.A. degree, I registered once more for Math 61 and once again faced Professor K as the instructor.

After the first session, I approached Professor K and tried to explain what I was facing. He answered with a sneer, "You know, Petrella, some people just don't belong in college." At that point, all the years of frustration took over, and I picked up a chair and attempted to throw it at Professor K. Other students inter-vened and security was called. I was literally "thrown out" of college. I continued to work at my day job and soon after mar-ried my wife, Margaret, in June, 1954.

In October, 1954, I was drafted into the army because I had lost my student exemption. While I was in the army, my first child Phyllis was born, and I had no clue as to what I was going to do with my life when I finished my tour of duty. I learned that I was eligible to continue my education under the GI Bill, but I still needed eleven credits for my bachelor's degree, and I was not welcome at City College of New York.

I was due to be discharged on October 24th, 1956, and in September, while still stationed at Fort Lewis, Washington, I wrote to Dean Barber at CCNY. In my letter, I explained to him that I deeply regretted my impulsive act and was now older, more mature, married and a father. I asked him to allow me to return to CCNY to complete my B.A. and move on to an M.A. with support from the GI Bill.

In early October I received a favorable response from Dean Barber and was informed that I could register for the spring term. In February 1957, at the age of 25, I returned to CCNY and still had to pass the required freshman course—Math 61.

There I sat in a classroom with eighteen-year-old freshmen, trying to pass a course that I had failed several times. I had not taken a college course in three years, and I was sure that I would have an even greater problem passing mathematics. The only positive factor was that my old nemesis, Professor K, was no longer the instructor.

The course was being taught by a young man whose name I cannot remember, but whose intervention at this time turned out to be the most critical educational experience of my life.

When the first session of his course ended, I waited for the other students to leave and asked if I could speak to him for a few minutes. He listened intently as I described all that had happened. I told him that I felt foolish having to sit with freshmen knowing that I lacked their skills. I described my insecurity about being able to pass the course. I told him that I knew I was going to fail.

He said empathetically, "You are going to pass, but you will have to earn a passing grade." He explained that he was an adjunct professor whose regular day job was with the Internal Revenue Service. He said that if I was willing to report to his office two days a week during his lunch hour, he would tutor me free of charge.

I accepted his challenge, and Math 61 became easier for me to understand. I received a final grade of B+ and was graduated in May of 1957. In September 1957, I began teaching in the New York City School System.

I became a Guidance Counselor in 1962, an assistant principal in 1967, a principal in 1972, and a superintendent of schools in 1985.

꿒꿒꿒 8 꿒꿒꿒

Insight

ELAINE ROBBINS HARRIS

ONCE YOU MAKE A commitment to become a lifelong learner, you realize that all of the experience and all of the people on your journey are there to teach you something. Some of the most meaningful learning takes place when you reach inside yourself to support a stranger through a struggle.

I will never forget Mildred and the impact she had on my life because I reached out to her. I was doing a training seminar for a group of corporate managers in a large urban city. The workshop was designed to support the participants in addressing their development issues so they could support their employees.

In any setting of this type, there is always a mix of participants with varying levels of interest and enthusiasm. There are hostages (individuals who'd rather not be there), vacationers/tourist (individuals who are just passing time), and the learners (they do not require definition). As any trainer or teacher knows, participants will reveal their identities early in the process. But as we moved through the process a comfortable familiarity developed in the room and a group identity evolved. We shared experiences, stories, and laughter. A stimulating energy filled the room.

As I scanned the room, I observed one participant who had detached herself from the entire group. She was not acting like a hostage by putting negative energy into the room—she had withdrawn all of the energy into herself and wrapped herself with an invisible barrier. In all honesty, I have to admit that my first inclination was to ignore her. She had withdrawn so deeply that I did not know how much time or energy I would have to take from the group to reach her. But soon I realized that was not the correct response. As soon as I acknowledged that, I was actually drawn to her. At break time, I approached her and engaged her in conversation. I encouraged her to participate in the workshop and inquired if there was anything I could do to support her.

Something I said must have touched her because Mildred shared a story that left me with a mix of emotions: anger, sadness, and frustration. She had been sexually assaulted by a member of her family. That violent act of abuse and the breach of trust created a lot of pain for her. But the most painful part of this was the betrayal she felt. Her family encouraged her to forget it and act as if it never happened. There was so much I wanted to say to her, but time would not permit. I gave her a few words of comfort and went back to working with the group. She responded to my concern for her, and she projected a bit of herself into the room.

At the end of the day I went back to my hotel room and I could not stop thinking about Mildred. I was moved to sit down at the desk to write Mildred a four-page letter. The thoughts kept coming and I kept writing.

In the letter I told Mildred that in this life we are all on a journey. Each of us will have a variety of experiences on this journey. What we choose to take away from each experience contributes to the quality of the remaining journey. Some of these experiences are pleasant, wonderful, memorable. Unfortunately, some of these experiences are challenging and extremely painful. The painful experiences are the biggest opportunities for personal growth. I told her that I imagined this experience was terribly painful and difficult. I also told her that she had an opportunity and a choice. She could choose how to respond to this terrible experience and go on with the rest of her life, and she had the opportunity for tremendous growth. I told her that we all have an awesome, God-given power deep inside and that she had to reach deep inside and use this power. She could regain control of her life, or she could let it slip away. I also told her that she didn't have to understand the family betrayal, but it was important to forgive them. Not forgiving them could cause her to be emotionally stuck right where she was. I told her that she would go through a healing process, and while going through that healing process she would not only heal but would grow if she chose to use the power within her.

The next morning I gave her the letter. She left the room to read it and when she returned I could sense that the message had reached her. She thanked me. It was the first time I saw her smile and I saw several smiles throughout the day. At the end of the day, she told me she wanted to stay in touch with me. We exchanged addresses. I sent her a spiritual inspiration book. I hear from Mildred periodically. She sends me letters and cards. She tells me about her progress. She is healing and growing. She went back to school and completed her master's degree, and she has gone back to church and is singing in the choir. She is devoting much time, energy, and love to raising her son. She says she feels like a whole person again.

I am thankful that I met Mildred. I learned from my experience with her. She gave me an opportunity to be a channel for a life-changing message. She also showed me what can happen when a decision is made to heal and grow.

꧁꧁꧁ 9 ꧁꧁꧁

Team Effort

DEIDRA K. PERRY

AS A JUNIOR ACHIEVEMENT VOLUNTEER, I commit one hour each week to work with seventh graders for a semester. My role is to work with and talk to the students about presentation skills, college plans, job interviews, and goal setting. While I enjoyed working with the students at Woods Middle School, it was a less-than-ideal educational environment. Many of the students came from low income, single-headed families and were the unfortunate victims of a weak school system and teachers who went on strike.

The most disruptive student in the class was Emmitt. Regardless of my enthusiasm and the class's high level of participation, he always had a chip on his shoulder. Class would begin the same way. Ms. Hartford would either check last night's homework or assign homework for that night. Afterward, I would work with the class on a designated life skill. This particular day, Emmitt was allowed to stay in class because he had arrived on time. His seat was right up front facing the chalkboard (literally) because when he sat next to other students, he picked on them. As always, he told me that he would not sit up and did not want to participate that day. I told him to lay his head down and that as long as he did not disrupt the class, I did not mind him choosing not to participate.

I began asking the class questions about last week's discussion as a transition into today's topic of personal budgeting. I asked the students about their support systems and their ideal allowances. Out of nowhere, Emmitt said. "I think I would do better if my Dad was here." I looked at him sort of funny, wondering why he was, in fact, participating and what he was talking about. I then continued calling on students and Emmitt repeated his statement. That time, he got my attention. I stopped the class and asked him to explain what he meant.

Emmitt explained to me that he used to care about school and his future when his father was around because his Dad stayed on him about his work. Some years ago, his father died. Ever since then, he had lost interest in just about everything. The class confirmed this and proceeded to tell me that he skipped school a lot and was pretty much flunking out. (Seventh graders tend to know everything about each other and take on the roles of parents, siblings, and teachers in the class). Furthermore, Emmitt missed the bus every morning (including the first day of school), skipped tutoring after school, and got put out of different classes everyday.

Emmitt told me that he got to school around 10 a.m. When school ended at 3 p.m., he went to the recreation center (instead of his tutoring session) to play basketball and stayed until it closes at 7 or 8 p.m. The man who locked the door of the rec center took Emmitt home. He went home, ate, and then went out with his boys until midnight or 1 a.m. When he came back home, he showered, ate again, and watched TV until 2 or 3 a.m. This had been his pattern the entire school year!

Many questions raced through my mind like: Where is his mother? Why don't the teachers care that he comes to school two hours late? Why isn't he embarrassed to tell the class this? Why is he telling me?

By that time, I was consumed with Emmitt's story. I wrote his schedule on the board so that he could realize how many hours he was wasting. The only way I knew how to help him was to get his classmates involved. In exchange for a pizza party, the class agreed to help Emmitt. At 6 a.m., Keisha gave Emmitt a wake-up call. At 6:30 a.m., Amanda called to make sure he was out of bed. He met Jessie at the corner of her house at 7:10 a.m., and they walked together to catch the bus. Throughout the school day, everyone encouraged Emmitt to go to tutoring after school. After tutoring, Emmitt still went to the rec center (because he did not want to walk home), but he studied while there and spent time hanging out with his homeboys. He went home and was in bed by 11 p.m. This was a serious compromise, and I gave in because Rome wasn't built in a day.

Over the next few weeks, all the students became excited about class. Emmitt walked right up to me wanting to know if we could talk about him one day. Once he smiled and said, "I like sausage on my pizza."

Our plan worked. The students told me that when everyone saw Emmitt walking to the bus stop on time, they enthusiastically welcomed him on the bus. Emmitt still needs tons of improvement, but he is on his way. To my surprise, I learned that Emmitt, of all people, had been elected class president! Hearing that simply blew me away!

I cried when I got into my car that day because I felt as though Emmitt needed people to care about him. In some small way, he got that.

PART TWO

The Impact of Expectations

Death and life are in the power of the tongue.
—PROVERBS 18:21

*T*HE SPIRIT AND WILL of a person may be greatly
affected by what others expect of them. High
expectations from an elder, parent, teacher, col-
league, or friend may inspire one to accomplish
much. On the other hand, low expectations from
those same people may yield poor, substandard
performances. The manner in which one's expectations are verbalized often has a significant impact,
thus "Death and life are in the power of the
tongue." Words conveying a negative message can
shatter a spirit, destroy a dream, immobilize a vision. Messages that express doubt, constant criti-
cism, low esteem are deadly. On the other hand,
words of encouragement, praise, and high regard
can breathe life into a person's heart and soul.

10
Sitting Up Front

YSAYE M. BARNWELL

I AM A NATIVE NEW YORKER. I grew up in Harlem and in Jamaica, Queens, New York. I am African American and, in the experience I am about to share, I learned two lessons at the same time; one positive and the other negative.

My father was a violinist and named me after one of the greatest violinists who had ever lived, Eugene Ysaye. My father began to teach me the violin at the age of two-and-a-half. I practiced and had a lesson every day (except weekends) until I left home to go to college. I majored in music in high school and successfully auditioned to become a member of the All City High School Orchestra during the last two years of high school.

The problem was that while I believed I was as good as or better than many of my peers, I was placed in the last row of the first violin section. That was a disappointment because it seemed as though the best players were usually placed in the first few seats or rows of their section and the weaker players were placed further back.

I struggled with this inequity for several months without recourse until the day that a world-renowned conductor, Maestro Leopold Stokowski, came to rehearse with us. While I don't remember what we were playing, I remember that it was a very difficult piece, and I had worked hard to play it well. For some reason, Maestro Stokowski asked each of us to play a passage of the piece individually. When it was my turn, I played it very well; so well in fact that he placed me in a seat in the second row from the front. I was elated. My feelings about my abilities were affirmed. I was taught by my father—a black man—and I was as good as or better than my peers. I floated home to tell my father what had happened. He was proud of me, and I of myself and of him. I went to the rehearsal the next week still excited by my victory the week before.

But that was short-lived. When our regular conductor took the podium and saw me sitting in my new seat, he looked perplexed. I was ordered to go back to my seat. "But Maestro Stokowski gave me this seat," I exclaimed. But it made no difference. I was ordered to sit in the back. How could this instructor think so poorly of me when Maestro Stokowski had thought so positively about me? Only a week before, I had felt so proud in front of my white peers and now I felt humiliated as I went back to my old seat.

In that week of my life, I learned that I was as good as I thought I was and learned that racism is not rational or compassionate. I have never forgotten these lessons. It was the first time I had learned them, but it was not the last.

≈≈≈ 11 ≈≈≈
It's Okay to Say It
JAMES COUNTS EARLY

WHEN I WAS IN SEVENTH GRADE at Florida A & M University High School in Tallahassee, Florida, I experienced a chilling and simultaneously liberating lesson. Many teachers and students have, no doubt, experienced the negative part of this lesson a few, if not many, times in their pre-collegiate and collegiate lives.

Upon reflection, it is amazing to think about how many thoughts and emotions rush into and through our minds and bodies in a matter of seconds when you feel that you have been "put on the spot." There is that sense of injustice, of penalty, even persecution, in those gripping few seconds between a question posed to you by the teacher, the authoritative voice, whom we are trained to not disappoint with indecision, or worse still, an incorrect answer, and your slow-to-come response, loaded with a tone of shame: "I don't know."

I remember painfully my pounding heartbeat in the midst of those frantic moments. The inner voice repeating over and over "I don't know. I just can't think. Why me? I don't know!" I felt the eyes of all my classmates staring at me. They were waiting with silent anticipation to hear what I would say.

From the memory of your student years, recall the unsettling classroom experience of the sudden queasiness of the stomach, dryness of mouth, and the dazed, stunned feeling in your head. It made you feel as though you had just been jolted or catapulted into another dimension of time—all because the teacher looked straight at you and asked a question, the answer to which you didn't know. Immediately, you enter a dimension in which, through the haze of numbness, you are aware of your classmates, yet you feel alone, exposed, stripped of the reassuring feeling of being a part of them. A sense of emptiness engulfs you. You are embarrassed. You quiver inside. Have you ever had that feeling? Have you seen it happen to one of your students?

One day in the academic year 1959–60, I felt like my entire life flashed by me in an experience that lasted less than a minute. In that brief moment a teacher, Mrs. Laverne Moore, posed a question that I could not answer. Almost immediately she sensed, or perhaps from experience recognized, my inner panic, my outward fear. She immediately lifted my burden and said, "Mr. Early, never be afraid to say I don't know the answer to the question!"

In an instant, I had felt trapped and then liberated, challenged and embraced, stymied and exuberant. I knew right away that I had experienced a lesson for life when the reassuring, authoritative voice of the teacher said it was all right to not always have the answer at your fingertips, or even know the answer.

Over the years, I have often repeated that story to our now young-adult sons Jah-Mir and JaBen. Today, I tell it in speeches and class lectures to high school and college students, teachers and professors. The answer "I don't know" became for me an acceptable part of a life-long journey—an incentive—to learn. Mrs. Moore became a model of how to teach, nurture, and instill confidence and a productive sense of self in students. I learned an easy lesson the hard way because I, like so many (and far too many still today), was taught earlier, although unintentionally, to consider my lack of knowledge (answers) as my identity, rather than as a reason to expand my awareness, ability, and social development.

⚒ 12 ⚒
Let's Not Meet Again!

ELEANOR HOOKS

FOR A SENSITIVE, STUDENT-ORIENTED high school guidance counselor, monitoring detention can be a distasteful experience. Let's face it, students are punished in detention for not following the rules. They are detained beyond the normal school hours in order to teach them a lesson about misconduct and breaches of both implied and explicit contracts. For many teachers and administrators, detention is an institutional component that is necessary to maintain order.

When I, a guidance counselor, was assigned detention in a high school many years ago, I reflected on the process and the expected outcomes. I checked office records to find that often the same students were assigned detention many times. There seemed to be a "club" of detained students who were repeat offenders, often for different "crimes." I asked myself, "What was the point of detention? What was the learning for students?" After all, I worked in a "school!"

My day for detention arrived. Quite frankly, I looked forward to it. Arriving early, I entered a relatively small room with moveable chairs and an imposing desk situated authoritatively in front of the chalkboard. Students noisily filed into the room, but quickly took their seats, opened their notebooks, and became curiously quiet. Like children with bad coughs, they simply accepted the distasteful cough syrup called "detention."

I waited until everyone was settled. No one acknowledged my presence, as if I was an invisible guard assigned to their familiar cell. A resigned silence fell over the room—such a contrast from the teenage banter that I had heard moments before as the students entered.

There was something so unnatural about detention. The habitual detainees were well aware that detention rules were: 1) No talking 2) Do homework 3) Work quietly 4) No food, gum, drinks 5) Strict obedience to the rules for one-and-a-half hours and 6) Failure to abide by the rules would lead to additional detention assignments.

When everyone had settled in for a moment, I spoke to the group. I introduced myself and announced that I expected them to learn from being in detention today. Some were startled that I spoke to them, as if they were too recalcitrant to be addressed directly. Some did not look up, apparently because the tone of my voice was not a command, but an invitation. I invited each of the students to put their homework and books away and to arrange their chairs into a circle.

Many were dismayed. Others seemed pleased with the apparent reprieve. I expressed my concern that they had chosen to be in detention rather than spending time with friends and family. I asked for a show of hands for any students who had been to detention on at least one previous occasion. All hands raised proudly and defiantly.

Assuming a seat in the circle with the students, I began a group discussion by establishing new rules. First, each person in the circle would share with others what behavior had caused him or her to be assigned detention. Second, everyone would listen carefully to each other, so that the student could receive peer feedback. Third, after everyone had received feedback, each student would be encouraged to publicly state alternative behaviors he or she would adopt to avoid returning to detention. I established myself as facilitator and asked for a volunteer to begin.

One student shared that he was in detention because he was caught smoking in the boys' restroom. Another shoved a boy's hand into a locker—for fun! Still another left class early to roam the halls. One girl insisted on applying makeup in class after being encouraged to complete an in-class assignment. Another student brought a firecracker to school. Still another student confessed that he talked incessantly in class, even with repeated warnings from his teacher to quiet down. On and on, the students revealed their transgressions.

Confessions were good for their souls, but the feedback was even better. Students offered rather poignant and direct feedback to each other. As students received feedback in the form of suggestions for improvement, alternative strategies, or just plain ridicule, I often noticed a change in their demeanor from physically active to calm and reflective, from jokester to advisor, and, behaviorally, from self-centered to other-directed.

They had made a transition from simply enduring detention to exploring ways to never return to detention. The focus had shifted, and the students were beginning to become attracted to the problem solving and recognition that resulted from listening and receiving feedback.

The detention time elapsed quickly, but two students had not had a chance to share and receive feedback. The students agreed to stay a bit longer, although urging the two students to share quickly. When everyone had completed the process, I thanked the students for their cooperation and insights. The students exited the room quietly, after volunteering to rearrange the chairs into the rows that were there when they entered.

Although I did it "my way," I was happy to see the detention period end. As a counselor, I enjoyed a more supportive role. After all, detention was still "punishment." I was gratified that the students seemed to learn something useful from each other.

Two mornings later, I arrived at my office to find a note from the principal. Mr. Smith requested my presence in his office. The principal and I had a good working relationship, so I knew that whatever the issue, we would be able to resolve it. When I entered his office, he smiled broadly, invited me to have a seat, and told me he had had a visitor late in the afternoon on the previous day. The principal wanted to know what I had done differently in detention and why. I explained that I believed that students could learn from any experience if they were given an opportunity to reflect on the experience and to receive feedback if it was available.

I explained further that a teenager's reliance on peers is a useful tool for problem solving with them. The principal responded with some interest, but assured me that I would have no other assignment to detention. He said, "We do have procedures!"

Mr. Smith explained that a boy named Harry had been assigned to detention with me the day before. Harry confessed that he had been getting into trouble a lot and that although he was going to try to control himself, he requested that if he should be assigned to detention again, he wanted to be assigned with "that counselor lady!"

〰〰 13 〰〰

Taught by an Angel

Florence Roach

Can you imagine having such a hunger and thirst for knowledge that you would struggle fifty years to get it? I can. And only because I was blessed to be born the second child of an angel named Katie Fletcher Roach, who began grade school at five and finished college at fifty-five.

Katie Fletcher Roach was born on August 23, 1908 in Robinsonville, Mississippi, long before the casinos came in the 1990s. She was born into a poor sharecropping family of eleven children, a mother, Silvia, and a father, Rev. James (Jim) Fletcher, who was pastor of the local Baptist church for many years.

I had heard the story many times about how my mother's quest for knowledge had led her on a journey that lasted fifty years, but I had never focused on it until recently. This fifty-year road was paved with extreme poverty. In those days, students had to pay for books, even in elementary and secondary schools, and educating black children was not high on anyone's priority list. Therefore, the little money that was available to this family of thirteen was most often not used for educational purposes. In order to go to school, my mother had to chop cotton, save money, take a class. Pick some cotton, save some money, take another class, and so on.

My grandfather was a self-educated man and loved books, but could not always afford them. There was something about the few books they had that seemed to allow my mother to escape to places beyond the cotton fields of Robinsonville and dream of being a teacher some day. Now you must understand that this was some serious dreaming, because no one in this family had ever finished the eighth grade. But that was no concern for my mother because her books and her God told her that it could be different for her if she would just hang in there.

Why a teacher? Well, teachers, preachers, and undertakers (funeral directors) were some of the best-paid blacks around. Also, teachers were smart, respected, and wore pretty clothes. Yes, that's what she wanted to be all right. A teacher. And nothing was going to turn her around.

There was such a shortage of black teachers in those days that my mother actually began teaching after she completed the eighth grade. She began teaching on what was called a D license, and as she completed more high school and college courses, the higher the grade of license became until an A license was earned.

After finishing high school, she enrolled as a part-time student at Rust College in Holly Springs, Mississippi. She would work all week and take classes on Saturdays. She would work all year and take classes in the summer. I remember spending several summers in Holly Springs while my mother was in school. I humorously remember friends and I collecting bugs for her biology class and getting paid a nickel for each bug. It was in the summer time and bugs were plenteous—we were rich!

After never having enough money, never enough clothes, never having any family support, never losing faith in God, and after fifty years, Katie Fletcher Roach graduated from Rust College with a B.S. degree in education. Katie Fletcher Roach was the first one in the history of our family to finish the eighth grade, high school, and college. And I, her daughter Florence (Flo) Roach, was the second. Since that time, many have followed, and we owe it all to this angel.

My mother was my first-through-seventh grade teacher. She taught all grades (first through eighth) reading, writing, math, science, history, in a small farm shack in the middle of a cotton field with no running water or indoor toilets. And yet, somehow, she managed to teach us more than academics. Katie Fletcher Roach taught us faith, love, compassion, courage, and, most of all, determination. We were all blessed to have been taught by an angel.

Sun and Rain

Mut Nefereith Amenechi

YOUNG PEOPLE NEED to be nurtured. Like flowers, they need sun and rain. They do not need to be demeaned and ignored. Not too long ago, I was a substitute teacher for the New York City Board of Education. Being a sub was like being a turkey in a shoot. It seemed as if part of the job description was to be abused by the students. I moved around from school to school, district to district, grade to grade.

One day I was sent to sub at a junior high school in East Harlem. On my first day I was anonymously squirted three times with a water pistol. Even so, I became a regular sub because there I learned an important lesson about how a good school administration supports all its teachers, including substitutes. At this school, the principal, his assistants, and the deans would not let the children get away with squirting a teacher with a water gun. The offending students were disciplined and their parents were notified.

I found that I liked the age group of the students. Although they were rambunctious and defiant, I loved their determination to assert their independence and individuality. I learned that they did not respect substitute teachers who just came into the class with a cup of coffee and stuck his or her nose in a newspaper for the forty-five minutes allotted. These students were bright individuals and wanted to know if an adult in authority had something to offer them, something to stretch their minds.

At this school I learned about how effective reading aloud and storytelling was for this age group. I learned that everyone appreciated a good story. At first the defiant ones would ignore my stories, so for them I made sure I had a handout or a sheet of word games. They seemed to like that. It kept them quiet and occupied. There was another group, of course (the girls), who sat in a corner discussing things that seemed to be extremely important for their coming of age. I gave them their space. I would tell stories to those who wanted to listen. If it was a good story, it wasn't long before it captured everyone's attention.

My fondest memory of this experience, however, was when I had to sub for the small special education class. It consisted of eight young men—seventh, eighth, and ninth grades combined.

I came into that classroom with my word-game sheets. The young men ignored me. They sat in a corner in the back of the room also discussing things that seemed to be extremely important for their coming of age, and I gave them their space, too.

They weren't calm about it, however, like the girls were. They were loud, profane, and threatening. They uttered every expletive I had ever heard in my life. They repeated the disgusting obscenities over and over and over again at top volume. I just sat at the desk, observing this scenario; perhaps, I WAS just a little bit intimidated. Then, a teacher, an elderly man, came into the classroom. He walked over to me and said loud enough for the young men to hear, "Listen; don't worry about these guys. They are a horrible, stupid bunch. Just get through the forty-five minutes and then you'll be all right." Then he left.

The boys looked at me and continued their loud and profane conversation. Another teacher came in. She stood at the door and said: "Are you okay? These guys are a bunch of animals. There's nothing you can do with them. Just read or something until the period is over." Then she left. The students continued with their antics. A few minutes later, another teacher came in and again told me in a loud voice about these stupid kids and asked if I was okay. I assured him that I was fine, even though by this time my blood began to boil.

When he left, I walked over to these young men. All of my fear was gone. I didn't even think about it. It was as though I moved on reflex or something. I spoke to them for the first time. I said: "Listen." They glared at me. I continued: "Three teachers just came in here and called you stupid. They called you animals. I'm sitting here watching you and listening to you. I know you're not stupid. I know you're not a bunch of animals. I know you are so much more. Don't let people talk about you like that."

The young men sat silent for a moment just staring at me. They went back to their conversation, but this time it was a lot quieter and a lot less profane. The bell rang. As they left to go to their next class, they turned to me, smiled, and said, "See you later, teach."

Of course I was assigned to that class again. The young men would walk into the room and say: "Aw-right! We got you as a sub!" Then they would warn each other, "Don't mess with her, that's my teacher!"

From then on, we would have small conversations, share a few stories. I never had enough time with them to assess their academic problems, but I was granted a moment to help those young battered souls. I learned one of the most important lessons of my life. What our youth needs from us, more than anything, is our belief in them. They are like flowers, and our belief in them is like the sun and the rain. They simply cannot grow without it.

≈≈≈ 15 ≈≈≈
Principal's Pet
DEBORAH WORTHAM

AFTER BEING ASSIGNED as principal of an elementary and middle school, I was eager to move forward into my new venture. On July 7, I called the school to let the secretary know that I would be arriving soon. Perhaps I expected a welcoming committee. Perhaps a group of community members or even staff members would be there to greet the new leader. To my surprise, there was a welcoming committee. It was a group of students who wanted to meet their new principal who awaited me by the curb. Was I happy! As I walked from the curb down what seemed like a mile to the front door, they asked questions like, "You our new principal?" and "Have you been a principal before?"

I told them that I was the new principal and that I had had experience being the leader of a school before. I guess having successfully met their requirements, I qualified for the next series of questions. A tall, dark, handsome young man stepped forward. "Hi, I'm Lonny," he said. "I'm in the middle school. Can you have the middle school name added to the front of the building?" As I looked towards the top of the building, I saw that he was absolutely right. The name of the school was incomplete. Three years ago, the elementary school was extended to include the middle grades, but the name was not changed.

Considering myself a professional fundraiser, I knew that it would not be hard to cover the cost of the installation of the new name. It was a matter of pride for the students to have "middle school" added to the existing elementary title. I agreed to have this request honored. Feeling relieved, Lonny, who was as tall as I was (nearly six feet), fired off another question. This one caused me to pause and think about his reason for asking it: "Am I in the slow class?"

By this time, we were approaching the front door of the incompletely-titled school. The students had graciously taken my book bags, and we were already beginning to bond. I can't start off on the wrong foot, I thought.

"What makes you think that you are in the slow class?" I whispered. When in doubt, I always answer a question with a question. This gives me time to think.

"Well," said Lonny, "I got into trouble a lot last year. I barely passed. I missed a lot of days from school. I didn't want to come to school because I would just get into trouble. My report card was not good. And, I'm in 8-3, that's the last class of the eighth grade. So, am I in the slow class?" Everything that Lonny said made me think that in a traditional school setting he definitely would be placed in the "slow" class. Suspensions, poor grades, and poor attendance; these are typically considered to be a principal's nightmare.

I hadn't even entered the building and yet I was holding an unofficial "press conference" with one of my most important constituents. What do I say? In an instant, my entire educational philosophy surfaced and hit me solidly in the stomach. The reason why I entered the field of education sat right inside of my answer to Lonny's question. He was examining me to see if I believed in him. He had the tiniest glimmer of hope in his eyes. It was as though he was wondering, "Are you the one for such a time as this?" I paused, looked him in the eyes and said, "No, you're not in a slow class! In fact we are going to stop this nasty habit of having 'slow' classes. In this school, everyone can be smart! And everyone is a star! Whatever kept you from learning, whatever caused you to miss school, whatever made you get suspended is going to change this year."

Were these just words, platitudes filled with air? Were they just another set of clichés? Did I believe? "Lonny, will you help me?" I asked. "Will you help let everyone know that we are going to succeed?"

With a big smile on his face he said, "Yeah! And, by the way, what's your name?" I rang the doorbell, and entered the school feeling empowered, directed, and on a mission. I had a job to do.

Throughout the course of the year, Lonny had become the principal's "assistant." He helped or studied in a room in the front office after school and during some of his study periods. He still managed to get into trouble a few times during the year. Since his mother was not involved in his life and his father's whereabouts were unknown, we had a few parent conferences with his grandfather, and he made steady progress.

It took three months for Lonny and the rest of the 750-member student body to realize that they were all highly capable and that they could get smart through hard work. This was the result of intense and powerful staff training from the Boston-area based "Efficacy Institute."

My walking into classrooms, asking for the "ones who believed they could get smart" to raise their hands, involved a growth process and a set of new approaches that created an impact which spread from one or two students to ultimately everyone raising their hand and truly believing they could achieve at high levels, that they could work to make this happen! Changing their belief system and the belief systems of those around them (staff and parents) was a task. But it was a task that I believed had to be done for Lonny and all the Lonnys of the school. When your belief system is truly altered for the better , then you can focus on real strategies for success. The entire school year was spent learning how to succeed, step-by-step, celebrating every ounce of success and working on things we needed to improve.

We made changes in more ways than one. The physical plant received a face lift. Lonny and his constituents and parent volunteers helped to repaint the school. We instituted performance-based instruction, classes for "coaching" students, and a Saturday Academy. At the end of the year, four hundred suspensions were reduced to forty-three. Student attendance increased from ninety-four percent to ninety-five percent. Staff attendance increased from ninety-three percent to ninety-six percent. A three-year decline in test scores ended. State test scores increased from twenty-four percent to thirty-four percent of the students scoring seventy percent or better on the "big test."

Lonny's grandfather cried at Lonny's graduation from the eighth grade. Dressed in a light beige suit, with his hair freshly groomed, Lonny crossed the stage, determined. He had over-come a stigma, a label of inferiority that gets dropped on millions of students early in life. This change required only confidence—from the staff, in Lonny's capacity to believe that he had what it took to grow stronger, and my confidence in Lonny's teachers to believe that they had in their repertoire what it took to find the strategies for student success. Lonny passed all of his State Functional Tests and gladly progressed to the ninth grade. Are you Lonny or are you responsible for the Lonnys of the world? Look for these children, girls and boys, they are waiting for you to help them break through.

≈≈≈ 16 ≈≈≈

The Company You Keep

DEBORAH PEAKS COLEMAN

THROUGHOUT MY SCHOOL YEARS, starting with elementary school on through my college years, I enjoyed a positive educational experience. I made good grades, and I remember having loads of fun throughout those years. In high school, one of the single most important factors that helped me achieve academically was interacting with friends and classmates who wanted the same thing as I did—good grades—so that we could continue our studies in college and, hopefully, make a better life for ourselves.

It seemed like an easy thing to do, but I could have easily been distracted and taken my eyes off the prize. Growing up in my neighborhood in Durham, North Carolina, in the late 1960s and early 1970s, there was drug abuse and all of the unsavory antics that went along with it. These elements were extremely prevalent. I knew many junkies on a first-name basis, persons who had once been in my social circle. These were the same girls and guys who used to hang out with me in the neighborhood park, the same people who used to enjoy our backyard lawn parties.

I liked to party just as much as the next teenager, but fortunately I knew when to draw the line between doing what is right and what is wrong. I'm just grateful that I had the wherewithal to know how to select positive people and have positive forces in my life. In hindsight, I can't really say if the choices I made were based on values, or common sense, or both, because some things were just so obvious and plain to see. If you hang out with drug dealers, junkies, and other negatives forces, you are probably going to become a junkie, a drug dealer, and have a lot of bad things happen in your life. Realizing this, I had to know my neighborhood friends "from a distance." I really did not want to be on a close, interpersonal basis with them, yet I did not want to totally ignore my childhood friends, so I kept them at a distance. We gradually grew apart.

In addition to drugs creating a wall between my friends and me, there were other things that determined the company that I kept. Things like attitude, expectations, and behavior. By 1974, my senior year in high school, I had learned that those guys who wore "Superfly" suits and drove those cars with the diamond in the back and the TV antenna hanging out the window were simply "eleganza bammers." They were not as cool as they claimed to be. When several of my girlfriends were still in awe of these guys and wanted to be a part of their inner circle, I drifted away from them. I realized that many of these guys were going nowhere fast, and I did not want to make that trip with them. Instead, I wanted to take an exciting trip to college! As it turned out, most of the people who were my closet friends during my senior year in high school went on to college just like I did. We encouraged each other during that final year and compared notes about admission processes and scholarship opportunities.

When I arrived in Washington, D.C. in the fall of 1974 to attend Howard University, I found myself having to carefully choose my friends again. In my freshman dorm, some of the girls were purely wild and out of control. They wanted to party in the valley every night or go to a club downtown, and on the weekend they wanted to go to the cabarets hosted by the campus fraternities. At first, I said, "Yes, count me in, I'm going to the party." But then I realized that I did not want to keep up with that pace; I did not come to Howard University to party all the time. Some of the time was okay, but socializing every night was keeping me from my studies. Sure enough, most of the "Party Queens" in my freshman dorm ended their reign at the end of the semester or the end of the first year because their failing grades did not allow them to return.

Consequently, I became friends with girls in my dorm and others in my classes who had good study habits and who were serious about getting an education, yet we got a few parties in too. We had created a good balance—we studied hard most of the time and partied hard some of the time. It was wonderful to be in the company of people who had direction, focus, and goals to achieve. It reinforced my desire to do the same thing—set goals and achieve them. This was positive "peer pressure." Our interaction did not result in fierce competition or negative influence. On the contrary, we shared positive energy stimulated by hopefulness, self-esteem building, collaboration, and mutual support to "make things happen."

The company that I kept flourished even more when I joined Delta Sigma Theta Sorority in 1976. A founding principle of the sorority is scholarship; therefore, its members are committed to academic excellence. The majority of my fellow sorority sisters were indeed committed to doing well in school. They served in campus leadership positions and volunteered in the community. Not only is Delta a sorority committed to scholarship and service, it is a sisterhood devoted to supporting and caring for its members. The sisterhood demonstrated in Delta, and in other sororities as well, is a powerful force where women are nurtured, groomed and encouraged to excel. In sorority life, you can find women in different kinds of careers enjoying various levels of achievement, with most members realizing exceptional accomplishments. Sorority life stimulates educational and professional development. I have had the pleasure and great fortune of enjoying the company of my dynamic Delta sisters for twenty-five years, and it certainly has mattered greatly in my personal and professional development. We feed off of each other's success; we encourage and support each other in fulfilling our dreams and goals; and we mentor each other and serve as role models for one another—showing the other how to succeed.

Today, in my professional career and professional life, I strive to continue to keep good company. I embrace the progressive people who I encounter and avoid toxic relationships.

⋙⋙ 17 ⋙⋙

Everybody Needs a Brother Named "Bubber"

H. Louise Lassiter

I HAVE A BROTHER WHO is called Bubber by almost everyone in the family. I have always liked, respected, and appreciated Bubber.

When I was really little, he protected me from a bully who stepped on my foot. I told my brother what the bully had done to me. He knocked the bully down and told him never to step on his sister or any of his relatives. My brother was smaller than the bully was, but luckily my brother was stronger.

Another occurrence that made me really, really appreciate my brother and helped me to realize that I was very, very special to him happened when I was in the sixth grade. The schools were all segregated. Sixth grade students in our district had to gather one Saturday morning at a high school to take a test.

During the testing of sixth grade students, junior and senior high school students participated in a festival. After the testing period, all of the students were assembled in a large auditorium.

The supervisor in charge of the testing began her program by waving a one dollar bill in the air. She said that if anyone in the audience could guess which sixth grader had made the highest grade on the test, they would be given the money.

My brother raised his hand and gave my name. The supervisor said, "You are right, young man." Then my brother said, "She is not smart or anything. She is just my sister."

As a child and later as an adult, I always remember how my brother had the courage to stand up and speak up for me. His faith, love, and concern for me helped me to be the number one student in my ninth grade class, the valedictorian of my senior class, and to earn a BS and two master's degrees.

In recent years, my brother encouraged me to organize a scholarship fund within our family. We raise money to help young relatives pay for their books and college tuition.

During my long career as a teacher and school administrator, I would tell my students about my brother. One day, after I had finished telling stories about my brother, a student raised her hand and said, "Everyone needs a brother called Bubber."

≈≈≈ 18 ≈≈≈

April

Cheryl L. Evans

HER NAME WAS APRIL. I was born in April. She had long brown hair, a pretty face, and an attitude. It was February 1986, my twenty-second year as an educator. I had been hired at a community college on the north shore of Massachusetts to direct a new program for displaced homemakers. I had trained women in leadership development for high tech companies, tutored elementary children, directed day care and early-childhood centers, worked in student personnel with college students, and taught in an alternative school in Newark, New Jersey, but I had not met April.

The displaced homemaker program was state-funded and was intended to facilitate the re-entry of women with little or no work experience into the workplace. I had been hired to recruit women, design a curriculum, develop internships, and then do job development. This was the first program of its type, and there was a lot riding on its success. I had been job-hunting for six months and was grateful to have the opportunity to demonstrate what I could do.

April arrived at my office one afternoon while classes were in session. She did not have an appointment and did not apologize for interrupting me. Her arrival was abrupt and she took the only other chair in the office and pulled it up to my desk. She did not ask for any information. She told me she had been sent to my office because she was on welfare and was told to find a job. In rapid-fire sentences she made it clear that she hated the people at the welfare office; that she did not want to be here; that she really wasn't like the other women on welfare, and she wanted to know what this program could do for her. I had twenty-three women already enrolled in Project Venture; they were parents, too, and most received public assistance. I had black, white, and Latino women. Their ages ranged from twenty-two to sixty. They were hungry for knowledge and struggled to renew academic skills that had waned over the years. Working with them was affirming and gave me the feeling I was actually making a difference in their lives, except for April.

April decided that she would come into the program just until something better came along, to continue her welfare benefits. She was clear that she did not need the personal growth classes and did not like the reflective assignments. It was made clear to her that she would have to complete the assignments like everyone else, and the Welfare Department required regular reports. She told me she wanted to see all the reports specific to her before they were made. She asked me what my "qualifications" were and where I went to college. She pushed my buttons.

I had been trained in the use of win-win as a strategy, and set about convincing myself that I could see beyond April's ego-driven behavior that I labeled as arrogant, egocentric, and controlling. I said affirmations while she was in my office listing her daily complaints. I would silently repeat, "The Christ in me meets and greets the Christ in you." She did not like the clothes the other students wore, she did not like the way the teachers spoke to her, she did not like having to take the "psychology of self" class, and she did not like having to pick up a form verifying her attendance in order to receive her welfare check. She loved her son, but she did not like being a single mother. She was angry with men and angry at having her life "taken away" from her.

I told myself, "I could play win-win with April, after all I was the one who had the training and knew that win-win took time and patience." I could see my trainer handouts echoing their admonitions to "bring out the best in others; know that power people are infectious; trust is fragile, and once broken hard to repair; power is expendable; and that I should hold a positive view of her." I decided that April was probably very high in personal power motivation and had no interpersonal skills. I was also very high in personal and social power motivation, which is one of the reasons I believed that I was a good teacher and trainer. I was succeeding with all the participants, except April.

April sat alone during the breaks and left the building at lunchtime. She sat off to herself in classes and, when small groups were formed, she used the opportunity to disparage the teacher and the program. She held no respect for me and was not reluctant to say so. Other students came to me with concerns about her, but I told them she was growing, as we all were. When each student was asked to complete a form indicating his or her preference for an internship, April did not.

I put long hours into writing, calling, and meeting local employers to convince them to accept our "Venture Ladies" as interns for eight weeks. I came early and stayed late and finally placed everyone, with one exception.

It was spring 1989, and I was preparing to turn over the reins of Project Venture and accept a position as a full-time faculty member. This was to be my final Project Venture awards ceremony, the emotional culmination of a profoundly gratifying year to be part of the process. We invited Venture alumnae from past programs and relished the news of each woman's progress and success. The last minute arrangements were being made when my division chair called to me saying that he had a surprise. I turned, and there she was, April, smiling, and actually appearing happy. She was added to the "testimonial" section of the program. When she came to the podium, she looked directly at me and said, "Thank you."

April was thanking me, and the moment proved challenging. I did not now what I had done to, or for, her. I felt warm and uncomfortable and on the verge of tears. All I had done was expose her to other women struggling with burdens different from, but as heavy as, the one she carried. All I had done was refuse to engage in a struggle with her over her insecurities and lack of confidence in her ability to turn her life around. All I had done was see her as a vital shard in the cosmic mirror, shattered at creation, and incomplete without her. All I had done was my job, challenging the fears imbedded in her, in me, and in our history. It would have been easier to stereotype her, to isolate her, to be angry at her anger. The path of least resistance was an old one; April taught me how to see beyond the behavior, and that was all I did. It was a rugged and challenging path for both of us.

April earned an associate degree and applied to college. She was accepted by Tufts University and was awarded a full scholarship. She was applying to graduate school at Harvard to earn a master's degree in counseling. She said that she would not have been able to do all this without Project Venture and the help and support she received from me. She admitted that she had an "attitude" back then and realized how difficult she had been long after she left the program. She said that she wanted to become a therapist so that she could help other women like herself.

It was 1991, and I was preparing to leave my position at the community college and relocate to Virginia to start a doctoral program. Times were hectic, and I was anxious about how to accomplish all I knew was ahead of me. I received a small envelope, an invitation to April's graduation party being held right in my own city.

It was a Saturday afternoon, and I was accompanied by the new Project Venture director to just "drop in" at April's party. We were determined to circulate and leave, being polite but not too visible. I placed my small gift on a table piled with the beautiful flowers and wrapped boxes that surrounded April's diploma, framed in gold, and placed in the center of the table. I stood, frozen for a second as I realized what I was seeing. April called her parents to her side and a toast was made. She introduced her son, now ten, to all those present, and then she called my name. She introduced me as the "person who changed her life," and gave me a long, warm hug. I stood, almost frozen, as I felt a wave of humility and gratitude work its way through my body. I choked and hugged her back. April, this was April, and we were crying together.

PART THREE

Unique Achievement

The brain is the best storehouse for wealth.
—BAMBARA PROVERB, AFRICA

O N ONE HAND, these stories show how ordinary people can accomplish extraordinary things. On the other hand, the stories are testimonies that these accomplishments could have been done by anyone who realized that their potential is their true power.

19

What Looked Like Cheating Was Really a Good Thing

Jack Daniel

Sometimes we learn, we survive, and we overcome despite ourselves. In 1960, I graduated "Magna Thank You Lordy" from Johnstown High School. My class rank, SAT scores, and cumulative grade point average did not qualify me to go to any institution of higher learning. However, being at least doubly blessed, the "powers that be" decided to start a program for a few "high risk colored" students by giving them a chance to attend the University of Pittsburgh at Johnstown. As one of two "academically high risk" students, I could remain enrolled if I earned at least a 2.0 (C) grade point average. Thanks to a few "gift" grades, I received exactly a 2.0 at the end of the first and second semester. Upon the advice of my academic advisor, and unable to find a job, I decided to enroll in summer school.

While wrestling with college courses in early June, an English literature teacher requested that I come to her office in order that she might go over my last written assignment. After her devastating critique of my writing, I refused to accept her advice to enroll in a composition class. She then remarked, "Well, you'll never be able to go to graduate school."

And I rejoined with, "I am not planning to go to graduate school. I plan to practice when I graduate."

"I thought you were majoring in psychology," she asked in a bewildered fashion.

I responded, "I am, and I already have the beginning of a practice. On Friday and Saturday nights at the Coke Plant Club, I practice for free drinks."

"You do what?"

"I practice psychology for free drinks. I have four women and two men who tell me about their problems, I give advice, and they buy me drinks. As soon as I finish my four years here, I am going to start charging some real money."

About an hour later, I learned that a psychologist holds a doctorate degree, and that a psychiatrist, among other things, graduates from medical school. What I was doing was somewhere in the realm of practicing without a license, and I was totally naive about the nature of a college education. In a bout of depression, I left the teacher's office and considered dropping out of college. I was not sure that I was going to last through the four-year baccalaureate experience, and, even if I did, my 2.0 was a long way from the 3.0 or better that I needed for graduate school admission. To make matters worse, my debt was rapidly increasing. A job in the steel mill seemed mighty attractive, and if the mill was not hiring, then the Army was where I was headed. And then, I got my first break in college.

I noticed that the white students seemed to be "cheating" quite a bit. They would cheat by marking their books in three different colors of ink. First, they read and underlined chapters of the book in advance of the teacher covering the material. If the teacher mentioned the previously underlined material, they used a second ink color to put a star by that material. If the teacher mentioned material which they had not previously underlined, they used a third ink color to mark that material. Then, when they studied for their test, they studied their notes as well as the material with the different ink marks. I had never in life seen such cheating, and I was appalled by the fact that they would dare mark in a book. My mother and father would have half-killed me with either of their belts had I marked in our family's Bible, dictionary, or any of the Sunday school books in our home. And to pretend to be able to read and understand the material with the devious ink-marks trick was beyond belief, too. But I did what I had to do.

I began to purchase books in advance, just like the white students. I began to read and underline them in advance, just like the white students. I even took time to study by comparing my class notes with the reading material. Heretofore, I had simply listened carefully in class, read as instructed, if I had the book, studied an hour the night before, and took the test. I ended the term with a 3.60, never looked back, and earned a doctorate at age twenty-five.

20

Helen Newberry McDowell

Going to School Is the Only Thing I Ever Really Wanted To Do

AS TOLD TO NORLISHIA JACKSON

IT COST TO ATTEND HIGH SCHOOL IN 1920, and her family was very poor. When she had an opportunity to enroll in a master's and doctorate program, she had to return home to care for her ailing mother and was then left with six younger siblings to raise. Still, she earned two master's degrees and has given tens of thousands of dollars in scholarships so that others can get an education.

With her mind set on getting an education, wearing her black and white gingham dress and black bows on three plaits, fifteen-year-old Helen Ellison arrived at Bennett College in 1920 from the small town of Abingdon, Virginia. Bennett was a coed high school then, and a high school education was not free. To attend would cost her her savings from cleaning an eleven-room house at twenty-five cents a day, the money from her father who had sold his interest in his family's home, and twenty-six dollars from her two older brothers who walked thirty miles to contribute their entire first month's salary of fourteen dollars each from their labors in a Virginia salt mill.

"That's why I help anybody who wants to go to school. Going to school is the only thing I ever really wanted to do," said Helen E. Newberry McDowell, now ninety-six and living in Washington, D.C. She was the oldest girl of fourteen children born to Lucy C. and Samuel Fletcher Ellison. Helen says they were "as poor as Job's turkey"—so poor that he had to lean against a fence to gobble. Her mother had dreamed of being a teacher and had only one semester to finish high school when Fletcher Ellison persuaded her to marry him—on the promise that he would take her back to school himself to complete her last term. A parried promise—a diverted dream. His justification for not keeping his word was that keeping a fire burning in a one-room school house and having to teach children of all ages and grade levels was too much work for a woman. Perhaps he saw struggling to manage a home, cooking and cleaning for a husband, and giving birth to and raising fourteen children more desirable work for a woman. This was not what Helen wanted for her life. That's why when she came to Bennett College, marriage was the farthest thing from her mind. But she was chosen for a wife on her very first day there. Fellow student, William Lacy Newberry, from Liberty, North Carolina, pointed her out in a line of girls saying to his friend, "I'm going to marry that big-eyed one." Newberry was nice, but Helen had learning, not loving, on her mind.

Helen concentrated on her studies at Bennett. Because of her high academic achievement, she was exempt from all but two semester examinations and was allowed to continue at Bennett for a two year teacher training course. She received a high school diploma and a teaching certificate from Bennett in 1924 and began teaching in Wilksboro at a brand new Rosenwald School. Julius Rosenwald was a wealthy philanthropist who funded the consolidation of the one-teacher/one-room schools for blacks throughout the country into school buildings with many classrooms, teachers, and classes from kindergarten through eleventh or twelfth grade.

When Newberry pointed her out as the girl he intended to marry, he meant it. In 1923, he asked her parents for permission to marry her and, although they consented, Newberry had to get a license three times before Helen married him in 1925. She thought marriage meant her life wouldn't be hers anymore, so she kept finding excuses. Her goals still were to get her master's degree and doctorate degrees and to have a career. But her mother persuaded her to marry him saying, "It is better to marry a man who loves you more than you love him because he will try hard to make and keep you happy." Helen's father was very affectionate toward her mother and often told Helen, who never learned to cook, "You'll never be the woman your mother is." She would answer to herself, "Papa, you don't know how hard I'm trying not to be." However, she loved her mother and admired her positive attitude about life. She even emulated her immaculate house cleaning habits and still washes her dish towels, even though they're not dirty, every time she washes dishes—"because mama did."

She and Newberry were married in 1925, a year after she finished college and they were married for fifty-five years. He died in 1975. Her eyes light up when she speaks of him, describing him as the best man that ever lived: "You couldn't help but love Newberry. He was wonderful and everyone was crazy about him. We spent some of the best years of our lives at Bennett and always told Dr. Frank Trigg (Bennett president 1915–1926) that if we didn't have but two cents left, we'd leave it to Bennett." She has been true to her word, often giving to her alma mater, and recently she gave Bennett twenty-six thousand dollars.

Helen continued to fulfill her dream of obtaining an education. She earned her bachelor's degree in education from

Howard University in 1930 and was lined up to attend Ohio State in 1931 for a master's and doctoral program, but had to return home to care for her ailing mother. When her mother died in 1931, she returned to Washington, D.C., with her six younger siblings to raise and educate. By that time, she and Newberry had been married six years, so with her younger siblings to care for, they had a child for each year of marriage. She told the children that they would have no luxuries, only the necessities of life and any kind of educational opportunity available—as long as they gave her no trouble. They could go to a movie on Saturdays but had to be home by five o'clock in the afternoon. They lived in a six-room apartment and turned the lights out at 9:00 p.m. in consideration of the electric bill.

Newberry was making fifty-five dollars a month as a dining car waiter on the Baltimore and Ohio Railroad, and Helen worked part-time for a lawyer while pursuing her master's degree. Newberry rented pillows on the train, and Helen provided pillowcases from the more than seventy-two she received at a linen shower given for her when she got married. Every soiled pillowcase Newberry brought home meant twenty-five cents, which Helen saved in a jar until she had saved two hundred dollars. This she used for a down payment on a $6,750 nine-room brick house at 1223 Irving Street in northwest Washington, D.C. Joy! Joy! How blessed they felt to have such a fine home:

> When I was a child, our bureau locked, but papa cut a slit in it for us to drop our pennies in to save. I learned at an early age the value of saving and would choose to put my pennies in the bureau over buying a piece of candy. I often heard papa say, "There's no bank like a dirt bank." I wondered what he was talking about. But when I bought that first house, I realized what a dirt bank is—real estate! That house was the goose that laid the golden egg!

Helen became interested in real estate investing and was very successful. An example of her real estate savvy is her buying a house for $35,000, which was appraised four years later for $205,000, and which she sold for $5,000 less than the appraised value. Of her real estate investments she says, "Now I live on the interest and give the rest away to help others get an education."

Always in school or teaching school, she received her master's degree in education from Howard University in 1932, and a second master's degree from Howard University in English literature in 1942. A committed teacher who was determined that her students would learn, Helen taught for forty-seven years in the public schools of North Carolina, Tennessee, and Washington, D.C. Some of her best friends were once her students. She recalls a junior high school student who could not even read "the cat sat on the mat" when she met him. Today he's fifty-four, and she says about him, "Everything he's done worthwhile in life he's done on my advice—from marrying, to the house I advised him to purchase over his original choice so that he could live in it and rent the other two apartments, thereby living mortgage free, to decisions about his children." The college graduation pictures of his two daughters are displayed in her living room and she provided a $10,000 scholarship for each of them—one finished Syracuse University and the other, the University of the District of Columbia.

In reflecting on her life, she says, "Everything I do, I do in the name of my mother. I believe I am finishing out her life. She was married on the 23rd of February in 1899. On February 8, 1900, my oldest brother was born. I always say that she had only three months of freedom between leaving high school and the grave."

Helen believes that knowledge is power and that if you're in school you should have a goal. She also believes that one should save more than one spends because it doesn't take much on which to live. You only need food, clothing, and shelter. Over-eating causes all kinds of health problems. She says that some of us are "clothes addicts" and that it is ridiculous to buy clothing on credit. Our clothes don't even wear out, we just keep buying more. She chuckles remembering how people would say, "Here comes Helen in that same blue dress." But it didn't bother her because the dress was clean. People would ask her, "What are you saving your money for?" She felt that she might live to get old and if she did, she did not want to live on charity. "I'm so glad I followed my own mind." She sums up her thoughts by quoting William Wordsworth, "The world is too much with us, late and soon,/ Getting and spending, we lay waste our powers:/ Little we see in Nature that is ours."

21

The Cheerful Giver

RUBYE H. HOWARD

THE JOURNEY OF LIFE takes us along many paths, and along the way we discover many interesting people. Many times, our memories dim and some of these people are lost from our thoughts. Every now and then, we remember vividly one particular person and a unique experience. This experience is one that has remained with me for years.

My journey as a teacher in the public school system led me to a Saturday morning workshop designed to build creative teaching strategies, to share experiences, and to develop leadership. The group was made up of different ethnic groups and multiple levels of education. There were high school teachers, middle school teachers, elementary grade teachers, and administrators included in the group.

The workshop proceeded and excellent presentations were made. During the segment where experiences were shared, one very modest teacher stood and began to relate some of the strategies she used and some of the materials she was using with her students. Her enthusiasm was evident, and interest in her success mounted as we listened. It was obvious that this teacher had some equipment and materials that were both unique and expensive.

Of course, there were burning questions in our minds and the questions came forth. The teacher was very gracious and calm as she answered each question. After several questions, the teacher was bombarded with a barrage of questions: "Where did you get the money to pay for all of this?" "Did you get a grant?" "Do you have a sponsor?" The teacher was somewhat stunned by these inquiries, but she smiled and with a kind, self assured demeanor she responded, "I use my own money, I have more than I need, so I share."

Those simple words worked their way through my brain and in that moment a realization was clear. This is what it really means to share. It must have been a thrill to be one of her students enjoying and being enriched and nurtured by a person who cares enough to go the extra mile.

I used this opportunity to meet her after the session. This is a person who worked her way through college and was helped and encouraged by many people along the way. The salary she made as a teacher was adequate and provided her with what she needed to be comfortable, so the money she spent was her investment as a teacher. The dividends earned were evident in her calm spirit. She was a cheerful giver! Yes, my priorities were evaluated and to this day I remember this modest teacher and practice the art of sharing my blessings because I, too, have more than I need.

22

His Dream Came True

DARLENE LEDOUX

BETO WAS BORN IN TOPPENISH, Washington, where his parents would travel each year to work as migrant farm workers. Migrant farm workers travel from state to state picking a variety of crops like lettuce, cabbage, potatoes, and corn. It is physically exhausting working under the hot sun, bending over picking the crops ten to twelve hours a day, but this was the only means they had to make a living.

Beto's family lived in Eagle Pass, Texas. Every spring they would travel to Fort Lupton and Brighton, Colorado, to pick corn, cabbage, onion, lettuce, and beets. After their work in Colorado, they would travel to Washington and Oregon to pick hop. After the crops were picked, they would return to Texas for the winter.

When Beto turned five, his grandparents moved to Denver because they were too old to continue to pick the crops. Beto and his family continued to pick crops for two more years until Beto was seven years old. Beto's parents, Roberto and Louisa, decided to move to Denver so that their children could go to school. Beto's dad Roberto valued education and wanted his children to get an education, so that they could have a better life.

In 1959, Beto's dad, Roberto Villarreal, died of a sudden heart attack at the age of thirty-six. Beto's mother was also thirty-six, had only a third-grade education, and six kids to care for. Monthly income for the Villarreal family was a total of two hundred seventy-eight dollars a month from Social Security and Veterans' benefits. This was all the money she had to pay all the bills for the family. She bought many of their clothes from second hand stores. Mrs. Villarreal realized that she, too, had to change their life. She sat the kids around the kitchen table and told them that life would change and that it was up to all of them to work together to make a better life for themselves. She spoke mostly Spanish and began to learn English, too. She also learned how to cook Anglo food for her family, foods like spaghetti and hamburgers. She became bilingual and bicultural.

Mrs. Villarreal committed her life totally to caring for her six children. She insisted that her four sons work for the family by doing chores for neighbors. They learned how to roof houses, repair car engines, plumbing, and remodeling houses. They would give their mother all of the money they earned except twenty-five cents which they could keep for themselves.

The Villarreal family lived in a small two-bedroom house in northwest Denver. After attending a school that enrolled Mexican students, the Villarreals moved to a school that was entirely Anglo. At their new school, people pronounced their last name differently. Instead of rolling the r's and making Villarreal sound royal and beautiful, they Anglicized their last name and said Vill-a-real. The students made fun of and teased the Villarreal family because they would eat homemade burritos for lunch and wore *guaraches*, sandals, to school. Kids also hid Beto's sandals during gym class. One day he had to walk barefoot in school for most of the day until his sandals were found. In fact, boys would chase Beto home and hit him because he was a Mexican. As a young child, Beto would get beat up because kids challenged his ethnicity. This confused Beto.

Although bad experiences occurred at his new school, Beto began to have some positive experiences, too. There were more opportunities at this new school to participate in school plays, the color guard, intramurals, and enrichment activities. He began to learn more about leadership, perseverance, teamwork, and surviving in a culture that was different from his.

Beto attended Skinner Junior High School, which at that time was a predominantly Anglo school. He continued to learn at school and participated in many school activities. Then he attended North High School. At North, Mexican and Anglo students came together from different junior high schools. In preparing classes for his senior year, a counselor scheduled Beto to take basic classes such as boy's social problems and cooking. Beto's mother became angry because she had higher expectations for her children and wanted them to learn academics. She insisted that her son take economics, psychology, and sociology. At her insistence, a reluctant counselor changed Beto's classes from basic to higher-level courses.

In high school, Beto was also an athlete. He ran track and cross-country and participated in all school plays. One day, a close friend invited Beto to go with him to Colorado State University in Fort Collins to visit his friend's sister. Beto was surprised by the college atmosphere. This experience opened his eyes about the possibilities of going to college. He never thought that he could attend college. He thought that college was for other students, not for him. Beto's counselor encouraged him to get a job with the city of Denver. However, Beto insisted that he wanted to go to college. Beto's talent as a runner earned him a scholarship in cross-country track to Colorado State University. Unfortunately, Beto was not prepared academically and socially for the culture shock of college, and he flunked out in his freshman year. He returned to Denver, attended a junior college, improved his grade point average and enrolled at Denver University. He didn't have money for college but received a student loan and was able to pay the tuition and fees. He earned good grades and graduated from Denver University.

Beto's undergraduate major was elementary education. He dreamed of being a teacher since the third grade when a special teacher encouraged him to be the very best student in his social studies class. Beto's teacher, Mr. Seeber, bent over him to answer a question as Beto was sitting at his desk. His teacher wore a white oxford weave shirt, a tie, and sweet fragrant cologne. Mr. Seeber accepted Beto for who he was and encouraged him to work harder. One day he said, "Robert, you have to read these books and study these events. You can do it!" Beto felt this special teacher was putting stones across a river so that he could cross safely. This gave Beto the encouragement to work hard and learn as much as he could so that he could realize his dream to become a teacher and the dream his father had to send his children to college.

Beto became a teacher in an inner city school in Denver, Colorado, Del Pueblo Elementary. He worked as a teacher for six years. After completing his doctorate degree, Beto then served as an assistant principal at Cherry Creek School, Englewood, Colorado. The following year, he became a principal. Beto is quick to credit the Cherry Creek School District for "blowing air under my wings and allowing me to soar as a leader." Beto has attended the Harvard Principal's Center, was a member of a delegation to China, and won numerous national awards as an exceptional principal.

Beto Villarreal lived his life surrounded by a loving and supportive family with high expectations. He came from a migrant farm worker family and had a dream to become a teacher. He became a teacher, a principal, and a national leader in education.

23

You Can't Box Me In

RUTH TRAVIS

I ENTERED EDMONDSON HIGH SCHOOL in September 1960 and was an outstanding athlete. I lived with my oldest sister and her seven children in a house that was not conducive to studying. However, I did manage to make good grades. Neither one of my sisters finished high school. Most of the young women in my community did not finish high school. There were no role models in my neighborhood. Even in my church, there were a few women who had finished high school but none who had graduated from college. So I entered high school with the determination to graduate and go on to college.

While in high school, I had some of my earliest experiences with discrimination and confinement. One of those experiences occurred in my bookkeeping class. One day the bookkeeping teacher said, "You colored kids are going to have a hard time. Instead of going to college, you should get a job." I felt that this teacher was placing me in a "box." However, way deep down on the inside, I was determined not to be placed in a "box" by anyone—including myself. I decided at that very moment that I would not allow anyone to ever tell me that I could not achieve because I was not smart enough. I resented this teacher for the rest of my high school days. But at the time I was only sixteen years old, I did not know how to verbalize what I was feeling. So my deep involvement in athletics served as an outlet for my frustration.

But when I started teaching at Northern High School in Baltimore in 1969, my former bookkeeping teacher was a member of the teaching staff there. He remembered me from Edmondson High School and was constantly telling other staff members that he had taught me and that I was a very good student. That was interesting since he had declared a few years earlier that I would not make it. Now I was not only functioning outside of the "box" but I was on the same level as he was. And, I had a master's degree and he did not.

I graduated from Edmondson High School in 1963 and attended Coppin State College, a local institution, for one year. I did not know anyone who had graduated from college so I had to make my own decisions. I chose Coppin because I heard that students were not as serious at some of the other schools.

While at Coppin, I had a professor who was very "prim and proper." One day during my freshman year, a group of students were laughing and talking as they walked into her class. It was a group of approximately seven people, but she singled me out and said, "Ruth Travis, you are an intelligent young lady, but you are so *loud*." I don't remember anything else that she said. I only remember that again I believed that a teacher was putting me in a "box." And once again, I resented her for making a statement that was judgmental, negative, and embarrassing to me. As a result, I began to talk very softly, especially while in class. I seldom raised my hand to respond to questions because I feared being too loud. Even today, I talk in a low tone, and people often have to ask me to repeat what I've said.

A few years ago, I saw this professor at a dinner party at the home of a dear friend who I call Aunt Mary. I reminded the proper professor that she had taught me at Coppin. She wanted to know the details of my life after leaving Coppin in 1964. So, in a quiet voice, I told her that I had graduated from Morgan State University with a bachelor's degree in education, that I had gone on to West Chester State to get a master's degree in education, that I had graduated from St. Mary's Seminary with a master's in theology, and that I was now teaching in high school and serving as the pastor of a local church. She was very surprised that I had achieved that much. Again, it was clear that I had not allowed myself to remain in someone else's box.

Even after entering the ministry, there have been those who thought that I could not make it as a pastor. However, for fourteen years I taught school—a task that included coaching, serving as department head, athletic director, and senior class advisor. And for six of those years I pastored two churches where I had to drive 122 miles, round trip, every Sunday and Wednesday. I don't know where or when I developed the I CAN attitude, but I have never attempted to do anything with the thought that I could not be successful. I have experienced some failures in life, but whenever I fail, I simply try again using another method or another process or another plan, never saying, "I can't" or thinking, "I don't think I can."

I raised five of my sisters' children and put one through college on I CAN. I went back to visit a former next door neighbor who thought that I would end up like my oldest sister who had seven children, is unmarried and uneducated. This lady used to turn her nose up at me because our house was not clean and there were so many people living in it. Hers, she believed, was the ideal family—wife, husband, and son. I deliberately visited her a few years ago, just so she could see that I did not turn out as she expected.

I cannot fit into the box that many others have tried to place me. Writing this story has made me realize that all of the persons I mentioned, who tried to put me in a box, should be given a round of applause. I realized that they put me in that box but forgot one thing: They forgot to put a lid on it. And a box without a lid is wide open to receive gifts. A box without a lid leaves room for whatever is in to come out. This has certainly made me realize that God had his hand on my life before I was even born.

Even today at age fifty-five, God is placing more gifts in my life. I'm still coming out of the box and using the gifts that he has placed in my life. I thank God for every box because each one has simply revealed to me another characteristic of this awesome God that we serve.

24
Dueling with Dual Heritage

CONSTANCE GARCIA-BARRIO

THE TIME WAS WHEN my son Manuel wouldn't give me a quick *como estas?* or a fast *adios*. "I was a biracial, bicultural kid," Manuel said. "Speaking Spanish was one more thing that made me different."

No denying that difference, with one parent from West Philly and the other from Old Castile. I'd met my husband there during my junior year abroad, way back before Noah sailed his ark. My husband's whole family still lives in Spain.

From the start, we spoke only Spanish with Manuel, sure he would pick up English outside. He needed Spanish to embrace his full heritage. When we took him to Spain at age one, he had no trouble getting acquainted with his grandmother, aunts, uncles, and cousins. With many trips since, Manuel had eaten his share of paella and clapped his hands to Flamenco rhythms.

And to spirituals. He had heard stories of his great-great-great grandfather, a field hand in slavery time who was sold away from his family because he wouldn't let himself be whipped. All three of us had attended family reunions in Virginia where Manuel enjoyed fried chicken and tales of his gun-toting great grandfather who helped build the Washington Monument.

But as he reached the preteen years, Manuel's dual heritage seemed a double whammy. As Manuel recalls: "I attended Quaker schools, known for their diversity. But there was a divide between the rich suburban kids and city kids like me. And my skin is olive, so I identified with the small group of black students. Even there, my color and hair made me different. I wanted to wear my hair in a high-top fade, or "box," but my hair was too wavy. I made a mixture of soap and water to stiffen it and wound up in the dermatologist's office with irritated skin."

Manual elaborates further about his being different: "One semester a kid from Ireland, a Pakistani, and I had gym together. Three outsiders. We would tell jokes amongst ourselves. I'd ask the Pakistani if he parked his magic carpet outside, and he'd say, 'Where's your green card, Garcia?'

"I couldn't do anything about my name or genes, but I could stop speaking Spanish. All the lectures about the value of second language went in and out.

"The summer I was thirteen, the tide began to turn. I spent a month with my Uncle Rafa (Rafael), Aunt Maribel, and Belinda, Arancha, Diana (their daughters) in Valencia. I worked at Uncle Rafa's factory. He and I would leave Valencia after nine a.m. and drive out to the factory. By ten a.m. I would be taking wood slabs out of an oven and stacking them up. It was part of the processing before the wood was cut for veneers for furniture and guitars.

"We'd work until two p.m., then have the big afternoon comida at one of the local restaurants. We'd go back to work at four p.m., then stop at eight. I liked working with the men, being able to talk with them, and understanding when they told Uncle Rafa I was a tough kid. Sometimes they asked me how to say something in English. The words came out garbled when they repeated them, and Uncle Rafa would say 'locos!'

"In my teens, it was a burden being different. Now, at twenty-five, I earn my living as a translator. Being bilingual is money in the bank. And my dual background is a plus, too. I think it lets me see two sides of an issue more easily, not a bad life asset."

My son had learned a great lesson.

25

It's the Spirit of the Thing

GLENNIS POWELL-GILL

IT WAS A BEAUTIFUL DAY IN EARLY JUNE. The atmosphere at our junior high school was filled with excitement and anticipation. In ten minutes the ninth grade graduation would begin. Parents, guardians, siblings, and community members filed into the auditorium sharing joyful conversation. For many in our inner city community it was the social event of the year.

However, I was in my office sitting at my desk with tears in my eyes. These were not tears of joy; they were tears of agony and grief. On the evening before, I worked late reviewing the standardized test scores for all of our students. In spite of the fact that this was the first time our school had taken this particular exam, I had been confident that our students would perform well because of our previous performance on other state exams. I had been wrong. Eighty percent of our students scored below the basic level in mathematics and sixty percent scored below basic in reading.

I wondered how I would be able to deliver a graduation message of pride, enthusiasm, and hope. Waves of fear, doubt, and panic washed over me as I worried about the future of the students, the teachers, and even myself. The voice of one of my counselors summoned me back to reality; the processional was about to begin. During the ceremony, I looked hard at each of the students. I hugged each one as they crossed the stage and received their diploma. Somehow, my remarks during the ceremony came across as inspiring and meaningful. As I now reflect on the situation, I am certain that I was not alone at that podium. God's spirit must have interceded for me.

When the ceremony ended, we all stood to recess from the auditorium. As I scanned the audience, I then saw a young lady named Cookie and I gasped. Cookie had come to our school within the last year after having some behavioral problems and conflicts with the staff and students in a few other schools. In the beginning of the year, Cookie had some minor encounters with me, but these issues were quickly resolved. She went on to do a terrific job in her studies; in fact, she was one of the few students who scored at the second highest level (proficiency) in both mathematics and reading.

But Cookie had been missing from school for a week. School counselors had been calling her home to no avail. I waved her over to me and asked why she had been missing. With tears in her eyes she blurted out that her mother had had a heart attack and died. I held her in my arms as she wailed, releasing tears of anguish and pain.

"Come with me!" I yelled as I swept Cookie off her feet. I ran to the vestibule where most of the students teachers and parents had walked. I realized that most of them had moved to the reception area or outside where they could gather to take photographs. I managed to get hold of my assistant principal, the keynote speaker for the day, a music teacher, and a counselor. I quickly recounted the plight of this young student and said to these few, "Lets have a graduation for her right now!" At that moment, with Cookie and that small gathering of staff, visitors, and a few teachers, I realized a feeling of absolute and pure love. All of us felt it. And they said, "YES! Lets have a graduation ceremony!" The adults ran over to take their proper places in the auditorium.

As our music teacher began the processional, my assistant principal and I walked Cookie into the auditorium and down the aisle. It was magic! During this second ceremony, it felt as though the auditorium was filled with people. Soon it was my turn to go to the stage and offer Cookie her diploma. As I approached the stage I turned around and my spirit soared. Three-fourths of the graduating ninth graders had quietly tip-toed into the auditorium to participate in the mystical communion of this ceremony.

I left school that day feeling humbled and ashamed. I was ashamed that I had allowed one set of test scores to impact what I believed about myself and the future success of our students, teachers, and staff. I felt humbled because the experience of sharing Cookie's grief taught us a lesson about courage, love, unselfishness, and unity. On that day I realized that we had moved to a higher level of living and functioning as a school community. By the end of the next year, through strategic planning and hard work, we had dramatically improved our test scores. We continue to improve.

PART FOUR

Perserverance and Hard Work

You deserve your best effort.
—John T. Chissell M.D

Education is a Ladder.
—Manuelito of the Navahos, 1865

*T*HE MESSAGE HERE, of course, is that people must never give up. The answer to a dilemma, the solution to a problem, a clever and useful approach, or a correct option is always available to us. And one of the pathways lies in the vast repository of the tremendous human and spiritual resources that are available to us.

26

The College Door

CAROLE G. PARKER

I IMAGINE EVERYONE DREAMS of an opportunity to tell someone who doubted their ability, who discouraged them and guided them away from a hope, dream, or desire that they were wrong, that their prediction was incorrect, unfounded, discouraging, and definitely unfair. It never occurred to me that I would have such a chance. I was a senior in high school, and my white male guidance counselor informed me that, based on my preliminary SAT scores, I would never get within ten feet of a college door. I was stunned that he had the gall to tell me I couldn't do something I hoped for. Of course, I had not originally planned to attend college, but that wasn't important. He was telling me I wouldn't be accepted and if I were, I wouldn't succeed. Numbers were on his side; statistically it just wasn't possible. Well, six years after that incredible conference, I, without specific intent, returned to my school as an employee, a school social worker. I arranged a conference with the counselor who was to retire in two months and shared the success I had achieved.

Not only did I get within ten feet of a college door, but I was now here as an employee to encourage others to do the same. His face gradually became deep red and he denied any recollection of such a statement. I informed him there was no motivation on my part to fabricate such a story and could identify at least one other person to whom he'd made a similar statement. His response, with deep resignation and an understated apology, was that he supposed not! I felt gratified! Not in a million years would I have ever conceived the opportunity to prove him wrong and get to tell him so face-to-face. But I did! I made it to, through and beyond the college door.

It was a warm fall, I was eighteen, tall, skinny, and had a tremendous overbite. It was the first semester of my freshman year of college. I really didn't belong. To say the least, I wasn't the most attractive young woman on the campus and was ill-prepared academically for college. In my senior year of high school, I had switched from a secretarial curriculum to a college preparatory curriculum. I recall having much difficulty with some of the courses. In fact, algebra almost kept me from graduating. However, I passed with a C!

I had left behind my mother, in a three-room apartment, who didn't want me to go to college, not to mention that it was three hundred miles away in Baltimore. Her parting words still resonate with me: "If you go and get into trouble, don't expect anything from me. I won't give you a dime!" Well, I thought, what could she offer me anyway. Yes, she had a high school diploma, but for the past ten years she had not worked and we lived completely on welfare. I knew she couldn't help me. Her words hurt just the same.

So here I was, attending a small historically black college, feeling out of place, and having chosen to be here because I wanted to get away from home. Maybe I would find a husband, someone who would take care of me.

My course schedule was a typical one. English 101, freshman orientation, intermediate swimming, general psychology, biological science and introduction to social sciences. These totaled thirteen credits. I originally had sixteen credits, but dropped elementary Spanish because the instructor refused to speak English. I attended classes regularly and attempted to get into the groove of the campus. Biological sciences stands out as one of the classes I had trouble with; however, it was the course that lead to my having a successful college experience. Class met three times a week, Monday, Wednesday, and Friday, I went to class dutifully and listened intently to lectures and took copious notes. The hitch in this process was the first exam. I hadn't studied. In fact, I had not even opened the textbook. I went to the exam hoping and believing my steadfast attention to the lectures and fastidious notes would get me over. I didn't even know enough to feel anxious. As I walked into the classroom, I noticed there were five rows of one-arm desks, and I took a chair on the far side of the room next to the windows and four rows from the door. I chose this seat to avoid being distracted by the others in the class and to be certain I could not be accused of improper behavior.

Mr. Berry, the professor, distributed the exam. To my surprise, after quickly scanning the exam, I realized I could not answer one question! I was dumbfounded! I felt lonely and scared. How could this be? Well, let's be honest. I had never cracked open the book! I then began an internal debate with myself: should I sit here for an hour in pure misery, faking the process of responding to the questions, or should I get up and leave the room? I wondered how I could get out of the room without getting caught by Mr. Berry. Surely, Mr. Berry would be able to see that I had not responded to any of the questions, and I would be in serious trouble. I sat and pondered my untenable situation. The minutes felt like hours, yet only about five minutes had lapsed. With quiet resolve I rose from my seat, walked calmly and quickly to the front desk, dropped the exam face-down, and fled the door. Alas, I was not fast enough to escape and Mr. Berry's strong masculine voice called me to return to his desk. That was the beginning of my success.

I was quietly questioned by Mr. Berry: "What is this?" (My exam.) "Why haven't you answered any of the questions?" (I don't know the answers.) "Why don't you know the answers?" (I didn't study.) "Why didn't you study?" (I don't know.) "What did you come to college for?" (I came to college to get away from home.) Mr. Berry was getting nowhere with his questions. Just imagine a mildly sullen teenager, caught in the act of doing wrong! He finally said in frustration, "I think you need to see a counselor. I have a friend in the guidance office. His name is Clayton Stansbury. Mr. Stansbury is a guidance counselor, and I want you to make an appointment to see him. He is a personal friend of mine, and I am going to check with him to see that you follow through. Now you go over there right now." I agreed. I am, if anything, obedient in the face of authority. I walked across the campus from Science Hall to the Carter-Grant Administration building which housed the counseling center.

I don't recall my first meeting with Clayton Stansbury, however, I do remember meeting with him daily for almost two years. At mid-term my first semester, I had a 1.3 GPA with a warning notice. Two things helped me. First, I received a notice that my scholarship would be withdrawn if I did not achieve a 2.0 GPA, and, second, Dr. Stansbury provided structure to my life on campus. Here's what he did: He created a color-coded schedule that I followed religiously. The schedule included a time to eat, sleep, play, study, attend class, and take care of personal grooming such as laundry, ironing, and doing my hair. I didn't make a move without checking out the schedule. I met with Dr. Stansbury and began what one might call intensive therapy, although I didn't know it at the time. I would share the experiences of my life to-date with him, pouring out my heart, hoping to heal, grow, and develop into a successful person. I used the schedule for the reminder of my first semester and all of my second semester. I earned my 2.0 but received another notice that I needed a 2.2 to remain in good standing with the college. So, I worked for the 2.2.

I didn't improve much beyond that until Chelsea Harold, a member of a popular Greek letter organization, challenged me to achieve an overall 2.5 GPA in order to pledge her sorority. By the end of my sophomore year, I had tasted academic success by achieving a 3.1, raising a 2.24 GPA to a 2.6. I didn't drop below a 3.0 semester average once that challenge was issued. In the spring of 1970, I became a member of Alpha Kappa Alpha Sorority, Inc., and in August 1971 completed my undergraduate studies and was on my way to graduate school back in

Pittsburgh. Years later, I learned that Mr. Berry never followed up with Clayton Stansbury.

Today, I'm an associate professor of business at a small Roman Catholic college in Vermont. I have a bachelor of arts in sociology/anthropology from Morgan State University, a master's in social work from the University of Pittsburgh, and a doctor of philosophy in organizational development and analysis from Case Western Reserve University. I share the credit for these achievements with a number of individuals, but especially Clayton Stansbury. To him I offer my heartfelt Thanks!

27

Learning Made Relevant

CHARLES AUSTIN

THROUGHOUT MY ACADEMIC YEARS, oftentimes I had to research subjects, going beyond the assigned textbook, to get clarification or attempt to actually grasp the lesson being taught. In college, I majored in biology and chemistry and minored in mathematics. My main approach to learning entailed listening to the instructor's lecture and taking notes, reading the textbook, and discussing course work with my classmates. Sometimes I engaged a tutor and, of course, I called on the Creator to send me a blessing—a passing grade. I found it to be a misconception to think that everything needed to understand the material would be found in the assigned textbook. NOT!

I was starting my second year of college and taking Calculus I, when I began having a difficult time understanding the concepts and formulas. I asked the instructor for extra help in an effort to grasp the basics. The instructor told me to keep working on the problems in the book. I responded by letting him know that I did not understand the textbook. The instructor then said, "Everyone in this class and most colleges in the country uses this textbook, what is your problem?" Getting no help from the teacher, I asked some of my classmates for help and received tutoring, but I still did not have a handle on the basic concepts of calculus.

It was midterm time, and I was failing Calculus I. My other demanding classes (Physics I, endocrine physiology, chemistry lecture and lab, and African history), along with working full-time at a supermarket, intensified the problem I was having with calculus. Thinking that I had exhausted all avenues in an effort to learn the basics in calculus, I became extremely frustrated. Frustrated, but not defeated.

One day I went to the library to study, and I started looking for books on math, calculus in particular. To my surprise, I found fifty or more books in various areas of math. From that selection, there were about fifteen books on calculus. I thought that if the assigned textbook for the class wasn't relaying the message to me maybe another book would. I started analyzing each book by 1) selecting a topic from my assigned textbook, 2) finding the same topic in the library books, 3) writing down and comparing how each text explained and solved problems, and, finally, 4) deciding which book explained the information in a manner that I could understand.

After comparing these books, I was amazed to find that a thirty-year-old book presented the information in a manner that was easier for me to follow. This book provided me with a basic foundation and explained and solved the problems in many different ways so that I could understand. The assigned textbook and the other library books did not thoroughly explain how each problem could be solved. My new best friend, the thirty-year-old text, also had good visual examples on how to solve the problems. That same night I monopolized the copier machine as I copied the entire book.

One outstanding concept in the reference book that really hit home for me was having examples throughout that applied calculus to real-life scenarios. Making the theories of calculus relevant to my life was enlightening. I had a new-found enthusiasm for my Calculus I class. I was excited about being able to learn the material, I started transferring these mathematical ideas to other courses, especially my African history class.

It was while studying my African history course work that I realized that the building structures throughout Africa required the knowledge of geometry, calculus, fractals, and higher levels of math. The pyramids, obelisk, layout of African living areas, religious items, African cosmology, music, medicine, art, and other expressions of the African culture had integrated math. I was further motivated to learn even more complex details about math because I read about how the structures in Kemet (today known as Egypt) were brilliant works of architecture.

I realized two important lessons from the challenge I faced with calculus—first, never limit my learning to one source for information and, second, make the subject matter relevant to my life by finding real applications. Making the course work relevant by relating it to my life brings the subject matter to life, takes it out of the abstract, and places it within my scope of understanding.

28

I Did It!

CHERYL SPARKLE MOSLEY

THE FIRST WEEKEND of June 1992, I went to my hometown in Miami, Florida. I ran into a young man who was a pure delight to see. This young man was standing tall and proud. He was casually dressed in a striped tee shirt, walking shorts, and sandals. My eyes lit up when I saw him. We gave each other a big hug and exchanged greetings.

"Where are you headed?" I said.

"Now, Auntie, where do you think I'm headed? To see you, my auntie who's the storyteller. Give up some more hug, Story Dove," he said.

"All right, Poppy! It's you! Come, let's ride," I responded. "I have a surprise to show you." We drove about three miles to the surprise. The surprise was the new house. My sister and her kid's house had recently burned down. Poppy had been staying with family members until his mother could find another house. He was not aware that his mother had found a house. When we pulled up in the yard, his face seemed to glow from the joy of seeing a dream come true.

"A home at last!" He said. He got out and ran to the door, rang the bell, but no one was home. We both walked around the house, peeped through the windows, looking at the various fruit trees. He started talking about having his buddies come over and clean up the big yard and about asking his dad to buy some paint to paint the outside of the house and fix up the yard. "The family can have the reunion at our house next year, Auntie," he said. "I'm gonna help my mother keep up the yard and get the fruit off the trees. And now my little nieces and nephews can have a place to play outside!" he said. "Wow! We can have my graduation party next year in the back yard!"

We went back to the car and waited for his mother to come. While waiting, he began to talk about his school goals and future career. He was very excited about going to the twelfth grade next year, the senior prom, senior pictures, class ring, graduation. What excitement was in his voice and in his facial expressions. Looking at him and how he had matured, my mind flashed back to not long ago during his early teen years. I felt he would never make it out of junior high school.

My nephew went through a phase where he had lost all motivation to go to school. Getting him up in the mornings was like trying to move Mt. Everest with your hands. He became very difficult in his attitude and his personality changed. He would leave the house and never reach school. His grades dropped to an all-time low. Teachers were constantly reporting him to the office and the principal. My sister was always going to the school about his behavior. He became a problem in the home. My sister had to constantly stay on his back. Other family members tried to talk to him. His dad tried to reason with him. Privileges were taken away. In spite of all the hard times with him, the family continued to preach to him that if he was to ever amount to anything in life, he had to do it himself. No one could do it for him.

We assured him that, although we loved him, it did not mean that we would sit back and let him get lost and become another drop-out statistic. The family went through a period of what one would call Tough Love. Tough love involved not tolerating his negative and destructive behavior. His mother refused to buy his school clothes for him until he straightened out his priorities, and the family discontinued buying him clothes and gifts as well.

After about two years of his attitude of "This is my life and I know what is best for me," he began to realize the road he was on was not as glamorous and popular as he thought. And his best friends were moving on to high school and he was left behind.

Finally, my nephew made up his mind to make a change for the better when he realized his behavior had made him fall a year behind his best friends. He had to catch up in order to earn the number of credits to pass to the eleventh grade where his friends were. Poppy decided to get a part time job for his school clothes and other necessities. He enrolled in night school and attended day school as well. He had registered and was ready to begin night school when he told his mother of his plans. He did all of this on his own. He continued to do this until he earned enough credits to get into the eleventh grade. He took the necessary tests that were required and passed. He was finally able to get into

Miami Jackson eleventh grade classes. He continued to work hard in school keeping his grades up and maintaining his job.

His parents, family, and friends were proud to see that he took the initiative to make a change and to become the person we knew he could be. My nephew was even proud of himself and what he had accomplished. It was not easy to do what he did within a year's time, but he did it. He passed his eleventh grade classes and was promoted to the twelfth grade. What a joyous time it was for him and everyone that knew him.

As I sat there thinking that next year this time I will be sitting at his graduation, suddenly we heard a loud banging on the car window. It was my sister. "Get out of that car and come on in," she said.

A few days later I flew back to Charlotte, North Carolina, feeling very optimistic about my sister finding a house and especially about my nephew's graduation. The following spring, my sister called to let me know that Poppy was very depressed because he had just found out that he was one credit short for graduation. He had worked extremely hard to complete all the requirements for graduation in June 1993. He had worked so hard. He was so disappointed that he would not be able to graduate with his friends in June. He had tried to ensure everything was in order, now this. The family had to reassure him that everything would work out. He felt he had let himself and his family down. He became very despondent.

I called Poppy. "Hey handsome, What's up?!" I asked.

"Oh, nothing much, Auntie, except I've got a problem in school," he said.

"What problem, baby? Tell your auntie; you know we can work it out together."

"Well, Auntie, the school says I'm one credit short, and I can't graduate in June, and that I would have to graduate in August."

"Poppy, do you remember how your grandmother, Big Dot, always said that the race is not always given to the swift, but to the one who endures to the end? Poppy, it doesn't matter when you graduate as long as you graduate."

"I hear what you're saying, Auntie! I hear you. My goal was to graduate in June 1993, Auntie, and I wanted everybody to see me graduate in June, especially my mother," he said. "Now I feel like I let everybody down; even you, Auntie, because you said you would make arrangements to come from Charlotte in June."

My heart ached for his disappointment. I responded, "Baby, first of all your mother is so happy to have a son like you. You have made her the happiest mother in the world, and the family is so proud of you for what you have done and for what you are going to do. It doesn't matter if you graduate on December 31, 1993. Remember, your goal is to graduate in 1993, so it doesn't make any difference if it's August, it is still the same year. Look, Poppy, now I know you didn't come this far to start tripping about a June versus an August graduation. Don't you know the key action is to graduate? Am I correct or not?"

"Yes, Auntie, you are right. I guess I was looking forward to walk in June. But I can still be happy that I will achieve my goal to graduate in 1993 even if I walk in August," he commented. "Now that's the positive attitude a successful young man like you should have. You'll be the first nephew in the family to graduate! Don't worry, whatever day you graduate I will be there, so don't worry about me," I said.

"Don't worry, Auntie, you're going to be proud of me, and I'll be a Miami Jackson General just like you and my other auntie," he said.

"I'm already proud of you, and I love you. I know you can do it!" I could feel that Poppy was beginning to feel better about the whole situation.

On August 18, 1993, he walked across the stage to receive his diploma with tears in his eyes. At the close of the graduation ceremony he shouted, I DID IT!

Higher Ground
The Making of Young Scholars
Freeman A. Hrabowski III

I REMEMBER MY FIRST WEEK at the University of Maryland, Baltimore County (UMBC) in the spring of 1987 as if it were yesterday. I had just completed ten years of administrative work at historically black Coppin State College, in inner-city Baltimore, and had made the decision to move to UMBC, a predominately white and suburban campus, because of my conversations with then UMBC president Michael Hooker. President Hooker had challenged me by saying that, while I had already made a contribution to the inner city, I had the chance at UMBC to do even more for larger numbers of students, both African Americans and others, because the university would provide a larger base of support.

It was during the first week of my new job as vice provost when I stepped off the elevator on to the tenth floor of the Administration Building, where the president's and provost's offices are located, to find hundreds of angry African American students occupying the floor. Unlike my circumstances at Coppin, where I knew the students and they knew me, I found myself not knowing any of these students and, quite frankly, not being trusted by them because they had only heard of me and we had yet to have any interactions. My first thought was remembering my role as a student-leader at Hampton University during the protests of the '60s, when I was very quick to criticize the administration and to demand our rights. Suddenly, I realized the I had become "the man"—the administration.

During those days of protest, and with television cameras continually rolling, the students and we (UMBC's administration) went through tense negotiations. I became painfully aware that many of the students did not feel good about either the university or themselves. And, despite their frequent references to racism and prejudice on the campus, what I found most troubling was that most of these students were not doing well academically, even though most tended to say publicly that they were doing all right.

The most serious problem facing us was that large numbers of these students had come to UMBC hoping to prepare to become doctors, and while white and Asian students were succeeding in math, science, and engineering, black students were not experiencing the same level of success and were bitter.

I will never forget meeting with different groups of black students, asking them who were the smartest African American students in science on our campus. What I found most troubling was that they talked about students who had earned Cs, at best, in upper-level science courses. Their typical response was that any black science major at UMBC who earned a C in genetics or organic chemistry must be really "heavy." I kept thinking to myself how sad it was that people talked with pride about earning Cs in science—low expectations!

To create a supportive environment for minority students in these demanding fields, we first needed to think about providing support for all students. Working with department chairs and faculty, we identified some solutions, including strengthening our tutorial centers, encouraging group study, and helping students understand how effort and time are required to succeed academically. Having examined the problem from a broad perspective, we were able to focus on creating a more positive climate for minority students. Our vision, in fact, was to create a cadre of superbly educated minority students who would become not only researchers and professors of science and engineering, but also science and engineering leaders and role models for the nation.

With help in the form of a half-million dollar gift in 1988 from Baltimore philanthropists Robert and Jane Meyerhoff, we started the Meyerhoff Program with the specific purpose of improving the academic performance of African Americans in science and engineering so that larger numbers would consider careers in these fields. It was especially important that Mr. Meyerhoff had a special interest in helping young African American males because he was tired of seeing such negative images of this group in the press. Key ingredients of the Meyerhoff Program included focusing heavily on African American culture, group study, tutoring (not simply to survive, but to earn As), mentoring, high expectations on the part of both faculty and students, and ongoing discussions about what it means to be smart, black, and a budding scientist in America.

Later, when we talked with students in the first two (all-male) classes of Meyerhoff Scholars, my staff and I challenged them not to be satisfied with earning As, but rather to strive for high As. Though these young men did well academically, none immediately earned an A in an upper-level science course. It was a few years later, when the Meyerhoff Scholars included young women, that one of the students successfully cleared the bar. I will never forget, in fact, being able to announce to all the bright, young Meyerhoff students at an end-of-semester meeting that one of their classmates — a quiet, shy, and brilliant young African American woman from Maryland's Eastern Shore — had earned an A in genetics, the first one earned by an African American in the history of the university. I found my eyes watering as I made the announcement, and as I asked her to stand, every young person in the room also stood and applauded because she was setting a standard for them and because she epitomized the notion that a diligent and strategic effort leads to great achievement. There wasn't a dry eye in the room, and I thought to myself, "They will be just fine."

Pinky's Daughter

JANICE JAWARA BISHOP

I WOULD LIKE TO SHARE with you an incredible story about a fascinating young woman. Her name is Andrea Moss and she is my goddaughter. Her mother Pinky and I were best friends in school. We vowed to be godmothers to each other's first female child. However, I did not meet Andy, as she was called, until she was in the third grade.

You see, her mother and I no longer traveled in the same circles. I had pursued a career in the military and Pinky had the misfortune of falling into a life of drug addiction. I had heard through the grapevine that not only was she addicted, but that most of the members of her immediate family were smoking crack cocaine. At first it was incredibly hard to believe. Pinky's family had been a strong element in the community. There were more than thirty of them who lived within a two-block radius. Her grandmother ruled the family with an iron hand. After grandmom died, the family fell apart.

Now the only adult member in Andy's house who was not on the pipe was her other grandmom, Mamie. Even the new babies in the family suffered from addiction and withdrawal symptoms when they were born. Everyone was affected. Everyone lived together in a three bedroom row house in west Philadelphia's bottom, a neighborhood that had a notorious reputation.

One weekend morning about a week before Andy's graduation from high school, she called me. She wanted me to come by her house because she needed to borrow some cash to help her complete her graduation requirements. I was surprised, because Andy never invited me to visit her at her house. In fact, I had noticed that she went out of her way to prevent me from having to pick her up at home.

I rushed over to her house. When I pulled my car up to the address Andy had given me, I thought that I must have made a mistake in writing the number. The building looked like it had been abandoned for a number of years. One of the front steps was disconnected from the house and open, exposing a crack that was wide enough for a small child to fall through. And the door had no door knob.

I stood there wondering what to do when two small children ran past me into the house. I knocked on the door and the same youngsters led me down the dim hallway into the living room. I stumbled when my shoe heel went into a tiny hole in the floor. When I looked more carefully at the floor I realized, to my amazement, that I could look through large cracks in the floor planks and see into the basement. There were no curtains or shades at the windows. Sheets and blankets hung across the bottoms of the window frame. Cardboard replaced a broken upper window pane.

Milk crates served as chairs that sat beneath a three legged table; the fourth leg was gone so the wall was the support that kept the table from falling over. The sectional furniture was dark and worn; it sprouted metal springs and cotton stuffing. Wallpaper was stripped from the walls. On the dining room table sat a broken, two-sided hot plate. It seemed like someone had been trying to repair it to cook an evening meal. And several children were there, sitting on the floor in front of an old black and white television.

Ms. Mamie, Andy's grandmother, was sitting in a broken chair cornrowing (braiding) a child's hair. I stood there trying to digest the situation. I was physically and emotionally shaken-up. Years ago I had been in the military and I had seen a lot of disturbing things, but nothing had disturbed me as much as the sight of how this family and these children were living. I stood there silent for so long that Ms. Mamie had to repeat herself. "You come to see Andy?"

"Yes. Is she here?" I answered but the words seemed to come from somewhere else.

"No. She's not here, but she is just down the street. Joe Joe, take your sister's godmother to her," she said. Joe Joe was about ten years old. He was expressionless and his movements were automatic. He did not speak, but as he was leading me out he turned his head several times to be sure I was following him. When we got outside he expertly maneuvered himself around the cracked step. I did the same.

By the time I met with Andy, I was a basket case. All I wanted to do was to go home to my perfect little world and collapse. Andy saw my face and realized immediately that I had been inside her house. We sat in my car and talked. I asked her how she managed to do all that she did. Why hadn't she asked for help? Andy is very active. She is president of the student council, editor of the school newspaper; she plays the violin; she attends church regularly, and she has a part time job. I sat there in amazement as she shared some of the details of her busy life.

"I keep my clothes and personal belongings at my friend's house down the street. That is also where I bathe and dress for school." However she slept at home. She refused to sleep anywhere else. She said that she was needed at home to help her grandmother with the younger children. While she was at home, she would remind her siblings and her other relatives that if they worked hard they could "get out of this hell hole." She told me not to worry or feel sorry for her. To comfort me she put her arms around me and kissed me on the cheek. "God-mother, I have a surprise for you, but you will have to wait a week or so for it," she whispered in my ear. I felt guilty inside. Here I was being encouraged by her when it should have been the other way around.

Graduation was less than a week away. I went back to the house to see if Andy and her family were okay. I knocked on the door and it flew open, but no one was behind it. There was a terrible odor in the place and it was very dark. Just as I was about to call for Andy two figures jumped towards me. It was my old friend Pinky and one of her sisters. "I like that watch and ring you're wearing. Have you got a few dollars we could borrow?" asked Pinky. These were not the sisters and old friends I had once known. Their voices were menacing. I became afraid and started to retreat to my car. On the way I almost fell down on one of the broken steps. They were in hot pursuit and, although they did not touch me, I still felt violated. As I pulled the car away I could hear them laughing and shouting, "Come on back! We were just kidding."

Growing up, I remember visiting Pinky's family. The household bustled with activity. There was always some meeting or gathering going on. Now it was different. There was just Ms. Mamie with six or seven little children running around the house, undisciplined and uncontrolled. When I returned to the house again, my husband waited for me in the car. Inside I found Ms. Mamie doing her hair while the children played or watched television. Andy was also there. In the midst of the chaos, she sat furiously writing, putting the finishing touches on a speech. That was my surprise. Andy was selected to be valedictorian of her class. She looked lovely. Her face was radiant, golden brown. She was focused and intent on doing an excellent job on her speech. During our brief chat I gave her some feedback on the speech. I said goodbye to her grandmother and the children. And I left.

When graduation day came, Andy's speech was fantastic. Her delivery was powerful. Because of what she said and how she said it, the audience gave her a standing ovation at the conclusion. Many in the audience knew about her humble circumstances. Andy urged the adults as well as her fellow classmates to stay focused and "not allow anything or anyone to keep you from reaching your goals . . . short term goals and long term goals." She mentioned that while "you may live in the ghetto, the ghetto does not have to live in you." She also said that "we should put God first! . . . and that we should make no decision without Him." It wasn't a long speech, but it was powerful.

Andy received a four-year scholarship to a local college, plus room and board, and a generous monthly stipend. An anonymous donor provided her with a car. She was going to be fine.

That was ten years ago. Recently I had lunch with Andy. She is happily married and is a practicing lawyer. But her greatest news to me was that everyone in her family, except for one sister, was free from drug addiction. Even her mom, Pinky, has gotten her life back together.

⧓⧓⧓ 31 ⧓⧓⧓

Determination is the Key

ALYCE PEAKS LITTLE

I WAS BORN ON APRIL 7, 1929, just before the Great Depression, the fourth child in my family. We were a sharecropping family of fourteen, nine daughters, three sons, and my mother and father. As far back as I can remember, I wanted an education.

At an early age, my Aunt Lola came to take me to live with her. She had three children much older than me, and maybe she wanted to have a baby around. My mother was always having a baby. So, I guess I was not really missed at home.

We lived in rural Durham County, almost to Orange County. I was about seven years old when I started school. I believe that I started later than age six because we lived so deep into the woods (rural area), that a school was not nearby and my family's mentality focused on sharecropping, not education. Somehow I learned about school and could not understand why I was not attending one. Finally, after I repeatedly inquired about going to school, I returned home to my immediate family so that I could start first grade.

I remember starting school on Hamlin Road and having Mrs. Swan as my first grade teacher. I finished first grade, and I think I skipped second grade. Oh, I loved learning. I loved going to school, and I hated it when I could not go! I went to school on and off, in between my sharecropping responsibilities and if I had shoes to wear. If it rained, I knew that we would not be in the farm field planting tobacco, which was the main crop in North Carolina, but I may not have had shoes or there were too many holes in my shoes to endure the rain. The cardboard inserts in my shoes did not hold up most of the time.

My daddy did not believe that a woman needed an education. He felt that it was our responsibility to stay at home and work in the tobacco field. But in my heart, I knew that there must be more to life than sharecropping. I felt that God placed me on this earth to soar high and to make the best life possible for myself. Share-cropping was simply not in our best interest. After performing severe manual labor, our family still did not have adequate means; we would borrow from the landowner to get crops planted and when all goods were sold, we still had nothing. I could not go through my entire life like this. God placed another reality in my spirit.

After going to school sporadically, I finally earned enough credits to become a high school senior. I did not work in the tobacco fields that fall. I went to high school with the hopes of going on to college. I was the first person in my family to complete high school. Times began to change and my younger sisters and brothers did go on to complete high school, too. I guess I was a role model for them. I graduated number two in my class, and I was very disappointed that my father did not attend the graduation. He did not think it mattered.

I would often go to the library and look for information about how to go to college. I found several scholarships for black girls. I received a small scholarship to attend a school in Raleigh,

North Carolina, to learn how to cook and manage food establishments. This was not my calling; I did not like it. I returned home to let my family know that I wanted to attend a four-year college. No one could understand why I wanted to go to college. I left home with twenty-five dollars in my pocket that my brother Waddell gave to me.

I enrolled in Shaw University, also located in Raleigh, and studied there for one year. That was the hardest year of my life. I met a lady whose name was Maggie White, who took me into her home as if I were a part of her family. I lived with her while I worked and attended Shaw University. During this year, I fell in love and was married. My new husband was also a student. When it was time for me to begin my second year of college, I did not have the money to pay for it. My husband continued his education, but I did not. He even continued his education by earning a master's degree. It seemed that my time would never come to go back and complete my baccalaureate degree. It was now the fall of 1950 and my first child, a daughter, was born and soon after my son was born.

After my children were raised and well into adulthood, I returned to college to complete my studies. In 1967, I began working as a payroll clerk at North Carolina College in Durham (now North Carolina Central University). As an employee, I was allowed to take one course per semester at no cost. In 1969, I seized this grand opportunity and began taking that one course per semester and aimed to do so until I earned enough hours to graduate. It was very hard to work full time and take classes too. As a part of the University's policy, I could take that one course any time it was offered, which meant I could attend class during my working hours. I was very excited and motivated about being a college student; I would sometimes take two courses per semester (with my paying for the second one). When enrolled in two classes, I had to go to class during regular business hours and in the evening. After working all day on a college campus in the Personnel Office, I would be exhausted at the end of the day, especially on the long days when I had evening class. I would go home and get in bed relatively early so that I could wake up at four a.m. to study.

Through a divorce, full-time job (and sometimes a part-time job, too), family responsibilities, and life challenges in general, I persevered until I reached my lifelong goal of getting a formal education which included the icing on the cake—a college degree.

In 1979, after ten years of taking one or two courses per semester, I was awarded a bachelor's degree in business administration from NCCU at age fifty. My determination, desire for learning, and encouragement from family members, especially my daughter Denise and niece Deborah (both of whom graduated college before me), helped me greatly to persevere. I am very proud that my daughter, an accomplished musician and educator, also earned three master's degrees.

Many of my brothers and sisters attended my college graduation, recognizing that I am the only sibling to earn a college degree and that I achieved a goal that was very important to me. I realize that college isn't everyone's choice and that my brothers and sisters have accomplished much in their various careers. As for me, I am a lover of learning and always wanted to learn and enjoyed gaining the knowledge that books conveyed. This is truly my passion, learning, because getting my college degree did not result in a salary increase at my workplace, yet it does yield endless possibilities. After getting my degree, I was able to pursue other professional aspirations. One such goal included gaining membership in 1982 in Delta Sigma Theta Sorority, a national service sorority dedicated to sisterhood, scholarship, and service.

After retiring at age sixty-two from NCCU, I am still eager to learn and face new challenges. A few years ago, I began a new career (part-time) at the Durham Police Department where I have learned a great deal about records administration via computer technology. Still learning, now at age seventy-one, I am presently enrolled in a Spanish course as I see a need to be bilingual in today's multicultural society.

%%%% 32 %%%%

Two Can Play This Game

AVERY H. COLEMAN

THIS STORY BEGINS with my mother, Effie Wilkerson Hearn, who knew what she wanted to do and had a plan for doing it. My mother was born in the small town of Holly Springs, Mississippi. Against her mother's (my grandmother, Alice Wilkerson) will, she married my father, John Lee Hearn, the son of a farmer.

Mama was very talented. She could sew, sing, and speak. As soon as she finished high school, or maybe before she finished, she started teaching school. She even taught my father, who was older than she was. But since his father, Albert Hearn, was a farmer and sharecropper, papa did not get to attend school often. Rural schools were open only four or five months out of a year because children had to work in the fields.

Mama married my father and they had ten children. During this time, she attended a normal school and taught the few months the students were not working in the fields. Mama talked one student's father into buying him the eyeglasses that he had needed for years. The student's grades improved and he was able to finish the eighth grade.

Mama taught grades one through eight in a one-room schoolhouse. She was principal and teacher. Although she had to travel five miles to continue her education, she still attended the normal school in town, sometimes walking, sometimes riding in a wagon or on horseback.

When the normal school closed, she started attending Rust College in the summer time and on Saturday. Her goal was to earn a college degree. At the age of sixty-two in 1947, mama accomplished her goal. She graduated from Rust College with honors with a major in English and a minor in education. After the rural schools were consolidated, she was offered a position at Sims High School teaching English, where she taught until her retirement.

As a result of my mother's tenacity, many of the students who attended that one-room schoolhouse went on to finish college—as did her tenth child, yours truly. One of my most memorable experiences while teaching in the Chicago Public Schools was when a student had been recommended by his teacher to be placed in a special education class, Educable Mentally Handicapped (EMH). The psychologist with whom I had become friendly knew that I had a problem with students being placed in special education classes because they were disruptive or their grades were declining without trying to get to the root of the problem. She asked if I would take him until she could place him if he continued to display EMH performance.

The student was in the fifth grade. I had the top fifth grade class. I took the student and did one-on-one teaching with him to see what level I could place him. Although he wasn't on grade level, I highly praised his effort when he worked hard. Some of the students worked with him on a one-on-one basis, also. He worked so hard that he had no time to disrupt the class.

When I requested a conference with his parents, only the mother came. It seems that the parents were divorced or separated, and the boy was angry with the mother. He didn't like the fact that the mother disciplined him and made him do homework. But when he visited his dad, he was free to do virtually anything he wanted to do. I was also able to get the father to come in and talk with me. I explained the situation to him and asked for his cooperation. I gave the father homework for the student to do while he was with him. It wasn't easy, but the student soon realized that no matter which parent he was with, he still had to do homework. He realized that his two parents, along with his teacher, had figured out his game. His grades greatly improved. He scored at grade level on the city-wide test and moved on to the next grade. Periodically, he would stop by my classroom to let me know how he was doing. He finished grade school and went on to complete high school. I believe that this young man has gone on to lead a good life.

𝍖𝍖𝍖 33 𝍖𝍖𝍖

Against All Odds

BARBARA BURLEY

GROWING UP AS A CHILD of a single parent in the 1960s and 70s was not easy. Young people today think they have peer pressure. Well, I'm here to tell you—so did I. My mom did not graduate from high school, dropping out at an early age to help raise her siblings. Then living in the south, my mom moved to Baltimore in search of better opportunities. Those new opportunities oftentimes meant scrubbing the floors of friends to make ends meet. Regardless of her not finishing high school, she required that we go to school every day and that we attend church on Sundays.

My mom was one who always made sure that our homework was done and done correctly. She would check my papers and always ask, "Are you sure this is right? I think you need to look at this again."

When I was in junior high school, I was teased for one thing or another. Your mom doesn't let you go anywhere. You think you're smart. I was very active in school, participating in declarative and extemporaneous speaking contests. The afternoon before one such contest, I was beaten up by a group of girls who had often teased me. My English teacher had to take me home. My mom was upset that his had happened. I told her that I was not sure who had attacked me, for fear of being beaten up again by the same gang. The only thing that I could focus on was that I must show them—I wasn't gonna let them stop me from being in that contest.

I went to school the next day to everyone's surprise. I got on that stage and gave one of the best speeches ever. I won first place, went to the state finals and the national contest. That was the beginning of the building of my self-esteem. It was at that point that I started to tell myself that nothing and no one could stop me from achieving my goals. I was still afraid of the bullies at school, but I learned how to avoid them.

My English teacher and I became close and developed more than a mentor-student relationship. She was able to instill in me the confidence that I needed. It helped me to survive. After high school, I applied for scholarships to several colleges and received a scholarship from one of the local colleges. By this time, my mom needed help paying the bills, and I did not want to be a burden on her. I did not attend college at that time. At the same time I was applying to colleges, I had a back-up plan. Just in case I could not go to college, I took the U.S. government entrance exam, passed it, and was hired as a federal employee. I started working with the intent of going back to school later.

I became one of the youngest contracting officers for the Federal Bureau of Investigation (FBI) and was sent to school to become more proficient in federal government contract law, administration of government contracts, and other classes. I am currently the assistant chief of the Contracts and Procurement Unit at the U.S. Justice Department.

34

Out of Practice

CRYSTAL GRANT

AS WE MATURE and our children grow up and move out of the house, we may find time for new interests to fill the void created by the "empty nest." Some people return to academia for various reasons and goals, others may travel extensively or do whatever their heart desires. With my offspring being adults and living in their own homes, my husband and I have more free time to do as we please. I chose to return to college to study religion.

Now I had not been in a classroom or an academic setting in quite some time. Yes, I am a card-carrying member of the AARP, and my college education was completed over thirty years ago. So I was indeed out of practice when it comes to being a student. Returning to college resulted in new challenges for me— less memory to store information in my brain, weakening eyesight, slowness on notetaking. The traditional-aged college student is pretty adept in these areas compared to an older student like myself.

At the opening of the school year at our particular Bible college, students young and old were excited about the challenge ahead of them. Before the first test on the course work, my classmates and I thought we were ready. Many of the older students were just like me—out of practice—as to how to study effectively. When the tests paper were graded and returned, there were many disappointed students in my class. We did not perform well; the most disappointed students were those who thought they had scored an "A" grade.

In a reversal of roles, the mature students were told by their young adult children that one must study to get good grades.

After all, they were not to waste tuition dollars. With parents now on the other side of the learning process, children were guiding their parents over the hurdles of learning. The children advised their parents to make flash cards, use index cards, and to record scriptures and facts on tape for repetitive study. Then drill. The drill consisted of listening to the recorded information while driving to and from work or in your home. Then you must keep listening so that the information gets in your mind and heart.

Many of the baby boomer students realized a positive outcome from their new efforts. Of course, praying and believing in those scriptures brought a revelation of the power of prayer. The outcome of using index cards as study tools for repetition of facts and listening to audiotapes resulted in a higher yield on tests and great personal satisfaction. It's a wonderful feeling knowing that it is never too late to learn, even when you're out of practice. With a strategy for achievement and mastering your course work, older students can excel in the classroom.

PART FIVE

The Storyteller's Circle

A good story told well can change a life.
—LARRY GRANT COLEMAN

*T*HE AUTHORS OF THESE stories are teachers and professional storytellers who have used hundreds of tales with learners and participants in performances, speeches, and workshops. All of the tales the storytellers tell here present life lessons about characters or real people who "work their magic in the arena of support and encouragement and mobilization" for others.

35

Don, the Little Dummy

BILL GRIMMETTE

DON WAS A VERY LIVELY CHILD. Wherever he "walked," he moved with the energy of a nuclear bomb. In fact, he never really walked, he sort of skipped-ran all the time. Everybody Don met got a vigorous high-five and a wide toothy smile that fit his face like a Benin Mask. No matter what happened, Don would present his big, broad smile and follow it up with a swelling giggle that ended in a deep, ground-rolling belly laugh more contagious than a yawn. Don was a good child who loved to play with the animals as well as plants. Oh yes, he played with the trees and the grass, the flowers and the insects. Don was full of life.

One day, Don was in his back yard playing with the cat and his mom was in the kitchen cooking. Every now and then mom looked out the window to be sure Don was all right. At one point when she looked out, she saw something that shocked her. She saw Don lift the cat and toss her into the air. The cat's head hit the tree and she fell to the ground. Mom was furious. "What is wrong with this boy?" she wondered, "is he crazy?" Mom couldn't know that Don and the cat had been playing this game all day long. Only Don would pick the cat up and lightly toss her into the air. The cat would grab the tree with her claws, climb up a little way, and then jump back onto Don's lap. The two would have a great big laugh, then do it all over again. But when mom looked out the window, the cat decided she didn't want to play this game any longer. So she put her claws to her chest. Don tossed her in the air anyway, her head hit the tree, and she fell to the ground. Now the cat was not hurt, but mom was enraged.

She opened the door and called out, "Don, get in this house right now with your dumb self!" Ouch!! Now that hurt! Don had never heard his mother call him dumb before. He walked slowly toward the house with his little back bent over like an old man. He looked up at his mom trying to explain but she shouted, "Take your dumb behind upstairs to your room. You must be crazy." Don put a hand in his pocket and a thumb in his mouth. When mom told him not to bring his lame-brained self down until she called him for dinner, a permanent frown came upon his face. From that day forward, Don walked around with his hand in his pocket, his thumb in his mouth, a frown on his face, and a big broken heart because he thought that his mother thought he was dumb. Don seldom spoke again. He never smiled again. He never played with the cat or the dog or the plants again. Don simply walked around in a daze, bent at the back with a hand in his pocket, a thumb in his mouth, a frown on his face, and a huge broken heart because "Now," he thought, "the whole world will think I'm dumb."

When Don went to school, the children began to call him "Don, the little Dummy." The teachers began to whisper, "You know Don's a little slow." Don appeared to ignore all of this and kept to himself.

One day in school, the children were given an IQ test. They were all gathered in the cafeteria smartly seated behind the tables. Don was there as well when the teacher spotted him and said, "Don, you can't take this test, honey. You must go down to the principal's office." Don stood slowly, put a hand in his pocket, a thumb in his mouth, a frown on his face, and took his big broken heart down the hall to the principal's office. Just as the test got underway, there was a fire in the building. The teachers gathered the children and went outside through the nearest exit, forgetting all about Don sitting alone in the principal's office. Don stood slowly when he smelled the smoke. He walked out into the hall and, with a hand in his pocket, a thumb in his mouth, a frown on his face, and a huge broken heart, he began to cry and muttered under his breath, "I don't care if I burn up in this dumb building. Nobody in here likes me anyway. They all think I'm dumb."

Then he walked slowly down the hall kicking the doors to the rooms as he went. He came upon the door to the cafeteria and gave it a swift kick and the door flew open. Don walked in and there were all the test papers still on the tables. He walked over to the first desk, picked up the paper, tore it to shreds, and threw it on the floor. He went to the second desk, tore up the paper, and threw it on the floor. He walked to the third desk, picked up the test and saw that it had not been filled in. So Don sat behind the table and filled in the answers on the front and back. Just as Don filled in the final answer, the fire alarm stopped and the children came back inside. Seeing this, Don dropped the paper, put a hand in his pocket, a thumb in his mouth, a frown on his face, and took his big broken heart down the hall back to the principal's office.

The teacher picked up the paper that Don dropped and saw that he had completed it. She decided she would send it in to be graded along with the others. Several weeks went by and finally the results came back. All the children in the school had done very well. But Don had scored higher than everybody in the school. Don had scored 200 on the IQ test. The teacher could not believe her eyes. She ran to the principal and said, "Principal, Principal, Don is not dumb. Don is a genius!" She ran to the teachers' lounge and told them, "Don is not dumb, he is a genius." She told all the children in the school, "You must never call him dumb again for he is a genius."

One day Don was walking down the hall with his hand in his pocket, his thumb in his mouth, a frown on his face, and a big broken heart when he saw a group of boys standing near the water fountain. Don turned to go the other way when he heard someone say, "Let's invite Don to be in our club." Don's back straightened up. He walked a little further and saw another group standing beside the lockers and heard them say,

"Hey, Don is all right. Let's invite him to the party, too." Don's hand came out of his pocket and his thumb came out of his mouth. Don began to walk with a new strut. He suddenly looked people in the eye as he spoke to them saying, "Hey May," or "Wave Dave," and "Yo Joe." Don stopped destroying things and fighting with other children. And his performance in school shot up. He went through elementary school at the top of every class. He sailed through middle and high school with an almost perfect average. Don breezed through college and went on to get his master's and Ph.D. After college, he eventually became the president of a major, multinational corporation.

One day, Don was being interviewed on television and the reporter asked, "Don, when you were young they used to call you 'Don, the little dummy.' What changed you?" Don said, "When I was young my parents called me dumb to punish me. So I began to feel dumb, to act dumb, and I performed like a dummy. But then one day, a teacher said to me, 'Son, you are what you think you are, not what somebody else says you are. If you don't like how you're performing, just say what you want to be and that is what you're going to be.' They began to whisper that I was a genius, and before long I began to feel like a genius, I thought like a genius, and I behaved like a genius. By year's end, I was performing like a genius. Now I go around speaking to parents and I tell them,

> be careful of how you use your tongue,
> in the presence of your young.
> Children become the best, by far,
> of whatever we suggest they are.
> I then say to the children, 'say what you want to be and
>   that's what you're gonna be!'"

Don told that story to the reporter, the reporter told it to me, and now I have told it to you. You must pass it on!

36

Miss Wunderlich

HUGH MORGAN HILL (BROTHER BLUE)

Note: This story was told on the "Spider's Web," a radio program of WGBH Radio in Boston. Brother Blue received a special citation "for outstanding solo presentation" from the Corporation for Public Broadcasting for this story.

DID YOU EVER FALL in love with your teacher? It happened to Blue. It was like this, you see. I was eight years old, and I hated school. I was one black button in a field of snow. You know how it goes. They called me everything but Blue. And I cried. I liked to died. My name was D in everything. D in readin'. D in writin'. D in 'rithmetic. D incarnate, you might say. All I'd do is cry 'cause I wanted somebody to look past my eyes and see somethin' in me pretty. You wanna hear a secret? In the middle of you and in the middle of Blue, there's some kind of magic. It's there for love. If someone don't love you, you can cry. You could even die. I almost did, but she come along. Like a rainbow song. She could look through muddy water when children cry and see the beautiful butterfly. Well, in school I was cryin' all the time.

I come home cryin' and Mamma say, "What's the matter, Blue?" And I say, "Mamma, let's play peek-a-boo." She say, "Come on. You're no baby." I say, "Mamma, kiss me once, kiss me twice. It'd be nice." You know how mammas do. When they kiss you, they mostly miss you. They be saying, "Blow your nose," and "Don't tear your clothes."

Daddy was seven feet tall. Like a brick wall. A bricklayer when he could get work. Didn't wear no gloves on his hands, you understand. He was a macho man. He had a trick, squarin' off my face. Gonna turn it into a brick and put it in a wall someplace. He say, "You're no baby." And I cried. That's when she come along. When I was dyin'.

Miss Wunderlich. Like an angel. On my first test in 'rithmetic, I got D minus. I cried. I almost died. She said, "Come on, Blue, give me that paper. Let's play peek-a-boo."

She's lookin' inside of me. She's sayin', "Blue, I love you. In you, I see a butterfly. Come on, don't die, don't cry." She took my paper, and she put somethin' on there like a kiss.

Oh! Somethin' happened in my head. I heard music. I fell in love with that woman. When I went to bed, I say my prayers. Then I did my numbers. One times one is one. One plus one is two. Miss Wunderlich, I love you. Two times two is four. I won't be late no more.

Next test, guess what I got. A plus. That's what happened to Blue. If they only knew what love can do. It can change you. I fell in love with school, with the ceiling, the floor, the window, and the door 'cause she was in there. I fell in love with the sky, 'cause it was blue like her eye. It can happen to you. All you have to do is fall in love with someone. Someone who can look through the muddy water in your eye when you cry. Someone who can see your butterfly. The butterfly in your soul. And you become what that person sees in you.

Well, I went through all the schools. And I went to war. I traveled 'cross the sea. I saw so much dyin'. I heard a man cryin'. He say, "I'm thinkin' of my mother tonight. And I can't read or write."

I say, "That's all right. Let's play peek-a-boo. I know a lady with eyes of blue. She taught me a trick. Come on, I'll give it to you. I believe in you. I see a butterfly in you. Don't cry. Just try. And I love you, brother to my soul. I taught that man to read and write.

When I come home again, I thought I was cool. I went to school to say, "Thank you, Miss Wunderlich." But, guess what. There were tears in my eye. I didn't want the little children to see me cry. I wanted to write on the blackboard, "I love you," to prove I could spell well. But I walked away without tellin' her that I loved her. What a fool was I. She died in the snow, you know. I loved her, but I never told her so.

Miss Wunderlich, I'm Brother Blue. I love you. I'm playin' peek-a-boo in the streets, in the jailhouse, in the hospitals, in the subways too, and I look in the eyes of the people I meet. I pray someday before I die, before I blow away, I'll save one life, maybe two, like you saved Blue.

Good night, Miss Wunderlich. Good mornin' too, I'm Brother Blue. I loved you in this life, in the next one too. I'm a story-teller, travelin' through the world. All I do is play peek-a-boo. Lookin' for the butterfly in the people I meet. I believe in love, Miss Wunderlich. And that's you.

▰◆◈◆▰ 37 ▰◆◈◆▰

Up from the Eagle's Nest

LARRY GRANT COLEMAN

SOME FOLK SAID THAT it was the strangest and most curious thing. But after they had seen it with their own eyes, well, they believed it then. And they all saw it, a little baby eagle with brown fuzz and a ugly wrinkled face frolicking among a clutch of chirpin' baby chicks. This little eagle would run and bump the baby chickens like he was one of them. But he was not. After a few weeks on the farm, this baby bird was already twice the size of the chicks.

Farmer R.J. Jackson had been hiking with his son Teddy in the hills near his farm. When they discovered an abandoned nest, they assumed that some wild animal had disturbed the nest because there were signs of a struggle. This lone unbroken egg was partially hidden under brush a few feet away.

As a learning experiment for his son and as an act of kindness, Jackson took the egg to his own farm and placed it gently beneath a "settin hen" among several other "settin hens" in his chicken coop. The hen did not reject the larger eagle egg and sat on it until it hatched. Out came a wrinkled baby bird with a small hooked beak. All the chicks on the farm were short and squat, but this little bird seemed to grow straight up as if he were stretching to reach toward the sky. His soft feathers were dark and wrinkled. And even though he was very different from the others, he learned to waddle and peck on the ground like the other baby chickens.

Teddy became fascinated with the baby eagle. He would quiz his father . . .

"Dad, why is he still living in there with the chickens? When are you gonna let him fly? He must know how to fly!"

The father doubted this bird would ever fly because it had never known an adult eagle. "He's been here with chickens too long. He'll probably never fly. I think he believes that he is a chicken. See, he walks like a chicken walks. It's too late for this one, son."

But Teddy would not accept this. "No, No. I'll prove it. If you let me I will get him to fly and be a real eagle"

During the next week, every day, Teddy put on cotton gloves and long sleeves and worked hard to try to get the eagle to fly. Teddy had named him Bo. But Bo just would not fly. Each day Teddy would sit on a four foot tall fence and he would hold little Bo up above a small mound of straw, and he would whisper, "Fly," letting the terrified bird plunge below into the mound of straw. With each attempt Bo would fall to the ground, "poof!"

During the next week they tried again without success. The situation seemed hopeless. But Teddy was determined to get this eagle to fly like he was born to fly, and after a few days rest they started all over again. In the meantime, Bo was changing, looking bigger and more different than the baby chickens everyday.

Teddy tried everything he could think of. He even sang a song to the bird:

> —Fly little eagle, fly.
> You can fly high,
> you can zoom through the sky.
> Get up there and fly.

Well, Bo was getting pretty sore with all this trying and falling. And even though it was a little bit painful as long as Teddy pushed him, Bo would try to fly. He was flapping and fluttering. Gradually, they both learned that more flapping made Bo's landings a little less awkward and a little less painful.

When it was obvious that Bo's wings were getting stronger. Teddy moved up a little higher into the window of the barn loft. There was a huge mound of straw below the window. But little Bo' was too frightened to look down to see how far it was to the straw.

> —C'mon, Bo'
> get out there and fly.
> You can go high,
> zoom through the sky
> I'll help you fly, just try—
> take an inch, then a yard,
> but please try hard.
> C'mon Bo baby, just fly.

Then one morning, several weeks after they had first started, they were in the barn loft and something caught Teddy's attention out of the corner of his eye. In the distant sky, there was a golden sunrise and a tiny flicker. A half-mile away a bird was heading toward the farm. The flicker became larger and larger and Teddy realized that it must be an adult eagle. Nothing else would move so majestically across the face of the sun. As the adult eagle approached the farm, the chickens panicked and began running and jumping all over the place. Even the pigs started squealing.

Teddy could see that the wing span of this bird was enormous— six or seven feet. Even he was a little frightened. Everyone and almost everything on the farm was afraid, that is, everyone except little Bo. His hooked beak and yellow eyes were locked, like radar, onto the movements of this enormous, graceful animal. He had never seen anything like this . . . and he knew in an instant that this was where he came from, that this was who he really was. The eagle circled the farm riding on a current of wind, and at that moment Teddy held Bo high in the air above the huge mound of straw. Now Bo was standing in Teddy's gloved hands looking first at the boy, then at the scattering chickens, then at the eagle, and with more courage than ever before, Bo stepped out into the air, and he seemed to float from the boy's hands out onto the thrust of a strong but gentle wind.

This time Bo did not flutter and flop down onto the straw, instead he was lifted up into the air and into the path of the adult eagle. He was not flapping, he was flying. The adult eagle looked at him as if calling for Bo to follow him up into the air. He flew up for the first time, high above that chicken farm, and he looked down at Teddy as if to say:

> Thank you for staying with me, for believing in
> me, for encouraging me. You were right.
> I'm not a chicken. I am an eagle, I am royalty.
> Once I doubted myself, but never again . . .
> Thank you.

Bo followed that adult eagle and disappeared in the direction of the mountains. After that day, most people in the country, other farmers and such, would pass by the chicken yard side of the farm and notice that the baby eagle was gone. And they would ask farmer Jackson what happened to that eagle who thought he was nothing but a chicken. And the farmer answered them saying:

> He found out who he really was and he went to live
> where he belongs in those mountains over there.

38

Small Miracles

Adventures in Storytelling

BOBBY NORFOLK

I AM SURE THAT IN the history of every storyteller who tells to young children, there are fascinating examples of what I call small miracles. These occur when a child has been touched in a cognitive or emotional way. I think of these as the breaking through of barriers—emotional barriers, barriers to learning, barriers to understanding. Usually the storyteller doesn't even know it's happened, but teachers, principals, parents, and counselors observe and report to us that something extraordinary has taken place, such as a remarkably long attention span exhibited by a hyper-active child during the stories, or the sudden blossoming of a verbal skill that has never before been apparent in a particular child.

The storytelling experience seems to take on a meaning that ignites the imagination and awakens dormant artistic or cognitive abilities. Some children who are deemed shy and bashful wallflowers demonstrate remarkable hidden talents in theater, comedy, and drama when given the opportunity to contribute to the telling of a story or to participate in a storytelling exercise led by the visiting storyteller.

Once I asked a young boy to come up and recite a series of tongue twisters to me. There were around three hundred children in the room at the time, along with their teachers, counselors, psychologists, and speech therapists. I always rely on intuition when choosing students to assist me on stage and, almost every time, that intuitive technique orchestrates a little story magic. This day was no exception. When the boy I chose walked up to the microphone for me to interview, he kept looking down at his feet. I asked him his name and he said it, never lifting his head. When I said, "I'm up here," in an attempt to establish eye contact, he slowly raised his head and gave me a strange, trance-like stare, looking into his upper eye-sockets.

The look initially caught me off guard, and I hesitated. All I could see were the whites of his eyes; the irises and pupils had completely disappeared. But I continued to instruct him, and he slowly lowered his head, returning his gaze to the floor. I called his name and repeated, "I'm up here." He slowly raised his head and looked at me. After repeating the instructions for the tongue twister, I held the microphone to his lips. He recited Peter Piper fluently and seamlessly, and when he finished, the entire audience broke into thunderous applause, acknowledging this child's accomplishment.

After the performance, a trio of therapists told me that they had all been holding their breath in suspense at what the child's reaction would be because he was severely autistic. They would never, ever have conceived of his even volunteering, much less performing so well in an assembly.

As storytellers, we can see the candle flames in the eyes of students as they journey with us in story, but many times we don't see the magic that story creates in the minds and little hearts that have had pathways and portals opened. As Susan

Strauss warns us in *The Passionate Fact* (North American Press, 1996), "When you use a hoe, the result is immediately evident and predictable. A story may take years of stewing in the listener's imagination before the listener says, 'Aha!' and the teller has a little control over what message a listener will derive from a story." That's true. We have no way of knowing when or if the "aha" will take place—but every once in a while, we are privileged to be present when it happens.

My wife Sherry and I tell a story in our book, *The Moral of the Story: Folktales for Character Development* (August House, 1999), that I think bears repeating here. Recently we were teaching a mini-workshop for a fourth-grade class in the Atlanta area when we witnessed an "aha." The class had been told a simple story and led through a visualization exercise in order to help them make the story their own. They were then sent off in pairs to retell their new story to partners. The classroom teacher and instructors circulated among the pairs, observing and encouraging participation. When we noticed that the classroom teacher was repeatedly drawn to one particular child, we asked if anything was wrong.

"Oh, no," she whispered, her eyes never leaving that child." It's just that I've never heard his voice before. He has never spoken in class, not since kindergarten!"

But the child was talking, animatedly and enthusiastically telling his story to his partner. When the class reassembled, we called for a volunteer to tell in front of the entire class, and that child put his hand up first. As he walked to the front of the room, his classmates cheered and his teacher wept. But he didn't seem to notice. He told his story fluently and calmly, as if this was the most natural thing in the world to him, and then he returned to his seat to wild applause.

Now, the teacher told us it was a miracle (so did the principal and several other teachers who had that child in class). And we later learned that the effect was a lasting one—he continued to talk in class and participate fully from that day on. Well, maybe it wasn't a miracle, but it was certainly an "aha."

"Aha"s do happen. The plot of the story, or the description of a place, or the sound of a voice, or the tilt of a head may have been the key that unlocked the door for that child. We'll never know exactly what happened, only that it did.

For every "aha!" moment that we as storytellers are privileged to witness, we know that there are hundreds more that we don't get to see: the witnessed moments are only the tip of the iceberg. We may not know when or why or how doors are unlocked for children through our stories—we simply know and believe that they are. And whether or not we are allowed to see the small miracles, we keep on keepin' on.

So, share the stories and allow the stories to work their magic.

▷◇◆◇◆◁ 39 ▷◇◆◇◆◁
How She Told Her Story

Michelle Austin

I can still remember that first week of my third-grade year. Our first assignment was to write a nostalgic story—one that reflected on our past—and at the end of that week tell the story without reading it off the paper. The first story that appeared in my mind was of a day a few summers before that I had spent with my cousins. We spent all day climbing trees, playing hide-and-seek, feeding cows, being chased by stray dogs, and playing in the mud in the orchard next to their house. I wasn't even nervous about speaking in front of my class because I knew my story all too well. I didn't even feel the need to memorize it; I would just tell my story just as I remembered it.

I was so anxious for Friday to come during that first week of school because I was excited to tell about my adventurous day with my cousins. I also wanted to impress the cute boy, Carmen, who sat a couple of seats behind me, with my storytelling skills. I anticipated the day while most of my classmates were dreading it; my friends were frightened to speak in public. When the day finally arrived, I was so eager to "tell" that I was the first person in my seat prepared for class. At last everyone around me was seated at his or her desk, and the final bell rang for class. The teacher rose from her desk cradling a red binder in her arms, which I knew to be her grade book. It was brand new with fresh writing on the cover: "Mrs. Rubert, Grade 3." I was overwhelmed because I thought she would begin alphabetically, like all teachers do with first assignments, and I would be the first to share my magnificent tale, but I was in for a surprise. She began with the bottom name and worked her way up. That meant I would be the very last student to tell my story that day. "Oh well," I thought to myself, "other people need a chance to be first once in a while." I just sat back in my uncomfortable plastic chair making an attempt to relax as I listened to my classmates' stories.

I was amazed at the stories that I heard. All of my classmates' stories were interesting. One boy used an instrument to add pizzazz to his story about the first music lesson he had ever taken. Sally, the shy girl, added a drummer's-like rhythm to her story about her vacation to Africa. Charles brought in a blanket as a prop to highlight the memory of being away from home for the first time at summer camp. But there was one story that really struck me. The storyteller was new to class, in fact it was her first day. The girl stood up in front of the class. She looked at the class with a bright smile and began moving her hands all about. She did not say a word. It was as if she were telling the story with just her hands. I watched intently, but could not understand. There were no words at all. "What is a story without words?" I thought. As I watched, I noticed the expressions on her face. There was so much detail to her story just through her facial expressions. I was so mesmerized by her graceful and swift hand movements, her face was like a movie in progress. When she finished, she didn't use the traditional "the end," she just bowed her head and walked to her seat. My eyes were still glued to her as she walked back to her seat. I noticed she had a little grin on her face. I did not understand the story, but all that detail in her face told me it was a happy one. I wanted to know more, I wanted to know exactly what she was doing with her hands, and why she chose not to use any words throughout her entire story. I knew I should approach her after class, but I did not know how.

This is when my teacher introduced her as being deaf. When my turn to tell finally came, I rushed through my story. I was the last person to tell that day, and all I wanted to do was get it over with. I did not even want to describe any events of my experience; I didn't even care if Carmen was paying attention to me. All I wanted was for class to be over so I could ask my teacher about the silent story. I was too shy to ask the girl about her story, so I approached my teacher after class. I asked, "Why did she only use her hands during the story and not any words?" Mrs. Rubert explained to me that Patty was deaf and was actually talking with her hands by using sign language. She was proud that I showed interest in what Patty was doing and that I had paid attention to a wordless story even though it was told in a new way called signing. I had heard about sign language before, but I had not given a second thought to learning more about it. I really wanted to communicate with Patty; I also wanted her to teach me to sign. For about a week I researched on my own, I learned the alphabet and a few basic signs. When I felt comfortable, I approached Patty by saying hello in sign. Patty smiled brightly and signed hello back. Behind that smile and in those sparkling eyes, I saw about a hundred stories unfolding, she would just tell them differently than I told mine, just as you would tell your story different from me. I guess this was a sign that we were going to be good friends.

40

Tales from the Couch

KEVIN D. CORDI

WE ALL SAT SPELLBOUND on that dilapidated old couch listening to my mother, and on rare occasions my father, tell us story after story about living in West Virginia. I would proudly take my place with my five brothers and sisters, and Mom would turn off the TV, and we would listen as my parents recounted their days of living in the Appalachian Mountains. The mountain people were not still, lifeless images on a page, but instead grand, larger-than-life movies that poured from our Ohio living room. I would learn about local folk-events like grandfather's struggle with the "biggest black snake in Clay County," or my grandmother's fear of the blind Fuller Brush salesman. I also learned the importance of tradition when my mother explained that the only way she knew it was her birthday was from the coal dust that her parents would place on her cheeks. On that couch, I learned my greatest lesson: stories keep us alive. Little did I know those "Tales from the Couch" would be my greatest tool as a classroom teacher.

In the fall of 1994, I was teaching at a new school, East Bakerfield High School in California. I had moved from the comfort of my hometown, finished a master's in "Storytelling and Education," and basically was by myself except when I was in the classroom. Students knew me as the teacher who told stories. Every day I tried to start class with a story, regardless of the class. Often the stories were "tales from the couch" or a folk tale or a fairytale that related to our instruction. On some days we just celebrated the joy of story by listening to each other.

In the spring, a young fifteen-year-old girl named Jennifer Wooley said to me, "Mr. Cordi, you love stories so much, why don't we learn them after school?" I was not sure what she meant, but she had a plan to start an after-school storytelling club. We decided to press on; we planned to tell ghost stories for a half-hour in a dark basement at the school. Little did we know that half-an-hour would turn into four in no time, and when the ghost stories ran out, we told stories on a new couch about their grandparents, their friends, legends, and myths from around the world. When the night was over, Jennifer gave us a new story assignment and Voices of Illusion was born.

Voices of Illusion is, according to the National Storytelling Network, "the first full-time high school storytelling troupe in the country." From that beginning we soon began to develop shows. Our first show was at the Tehachapi Wind Fair; a group of twelve students created a forty-minute show based on the wind. We began to meet weekly and spin new tales. We began to tell stories to the elders of Kern County, we traded stories with the young, the old, and with people who had never experienced the joy of a story told. I began to see a connection; I began to listen to tales of parents telling me how they were going to tell more stories to their children. I learned with every new story told by my troupe and me—the couch was growing.

In 1996, I was asked to start similar programs in a nearby high school. Since I felt like this was moving again, I began to explore new schools in other districts as well. Hanford High School contacted me and said they were impressed that I was a professional storyteller and teacher and would I consider teaching storytelling at their school? I was ecstatic at the prospect. When I arrived, I was informed that they did not want a class, but instead only an after-school offering. I refused to come until storytelling was a class and a club. I knew that telling stories in a classroom was too important not to be done. After a month of changing the master schedule, no small feat, they offered me a storytelling class.

Even though we have grown like wildfire, the real awards are in those moments on our storytelling couch. Time can not erase the moments when Shannon Angel and her family entrusted me with helping her tell the stories of her great uncle, the late well-known actor and Salish elder Chief Dan George. Or the face of Jose Gonzales when he flew his first time anywhere as we helped build a storytelling club in New Mexico.

The joy of Michelle Austin when she learned that she did not have to just write stories, she could tell them. Listening to Dawn Escobar as she talked about her passion for telling the story of Maria Mitchell, the first woman astronomer. Kelly Rutledge's musical accompaniment as she told an original story of John Philip Sousa. Gwen Green's wonderful letter thanking me for explaining how the tradition of saying goodbye is important to all of our lives. The tears of joy that the school cook had when she told of meeting César Chávez.

I often enjoy watching the faces of my students as they received praise for their work. The countless smiles, the safe place in the stillness, often to way into the night, telling story after story and always feeling comfortable that our metaphorical story couch allows room for everyone.

As the Irish saying goes, "Storytelling lengthens the road." How was I to know that my road would be a couch where everyone could sit down, tell their story, and stay awhile.

 41

The Desert Traveler

TEJUMOLA F. OLOGBONI

NOTE: WHEN I WAS A YOUNG MAN, I caused my share of problems. I was told by two different principals in two different cities that I was the worst student they'd ever seen. When I was in the eighth grade, a speaker at my school told this story (though a much shorter version). It really struck me. So deeply that I never forgot it. When I did graduate from high school, I graduated an honor student. On that day I was happy. And I was sad. Now, when I speak at schools, I tell this story. I see some of these former students, many years later. They tell me they have never forgotten this story.

Now, here's the story:

There were three men on camel, riding across the desert. The camels walked with a steady, rhythmic pace. The rider swayed side to side with each long, graceful stride of the camels. The creeping desert wind hugged the ground. Blowing over the camels' hooves as they walked steadily forward. The wind moved serpent-like, with a soft hiss, slithering over the sand dunes like so many snakes, swirling, here and there twirling a little dust column up into the air.

The sand dunes stretched seemingly forever. Sand. A world of sand, all the way to the horizon. Just sand. You see, there are no landmarks in the desert. The dunes never remain the same. They shift ever so slightly, unseeable, undetectable to the human eye.

The sun, high in the sky, was harsh and beautiful. Each of the travelers, as desert travelers do, thought of a nice, shady oasis where they could rest and drink cool water.

Their thoughts were interrupted by a voice, "Stop!"

The second rider said, "Did you hear something? What are we gonna do? Should we do something?"

The third rider said, "Be cool. That's just the desert wind. Let's keep riding."

The three kept riding, thinking about the oasis, when the voice again spoke, "STOP!"

"Did you hear something?" said the second rider, " What'll we do?"

"Man, I keep saying to be cool," said the first rider, "That's just the desert wind playing tricks on your mind. Why don't you guys just be cool?"

"Hey! I heard it say, 'Stop!' And I'm stoppin! Whoa! camel!"

The three riders stopped. The voice said, "Get off your camels."

"Are you gonna get off? Should I? What should I do?"

"Man, I don't know why I let you two hang around with me. Y'all just ain't cool. I don't know why you lettin' the desert wind run your life."

"Y'all do what you want! I heard the voice! I'm gettin' off this camel!"

The three of them made their camel sit and they climbed off.

The voice said, "There is a sand dune to your right. Go over that sand dune. There you will find a river."

"Hey, are you gonna go? Are we going? You think I . . . ," said the second rider.

"Hold on," said the first rider. "This is a desert. The definition of a desert is a place that doesn't have water. Let's get out of here."

"I heard it say 'stop and get off your camels and go over the sand dune!' Do what you want to, I'm goin'!"

They all went over the sand dune and there it was. A river. In the desert.

The voice said, "You will find pebbles in the river. Pick them up. Take them with you."

"First of all, I am too cool to be carrying rocks around in my pockets," The first rider walked over to the little river. He looked down, watching the cool, clear water flowing over the smooth pebbles. He hesitated a moment, then reached down and picked up three small stones, slipped them into his pocket, and walked back over to the other two riders.

"Did you get some?" said the second rider. "How many did you get? What do you think I should do?" He walked over to the river, stuck his hand in the water, grabbed a handful of stones, put them in his pocket and walked back.

The third rider shouted, "Hey! I heard the voice! I heard it talking! I'm not taking any chances, whatsoever!" He walked over to the river, reached in again and again, picking up handful after handful, filling both pockets. He was so loaded with stones, he had to use great effort to get back to the others.

Then they heard the voice say, "*You will be happy and you will be sad.*" Then the voice faded away into the whispering wind slithering, serpentine, across the sand.

"The sun will be down in a little while. Let's water the camels, quit all this fooling around, and get on to the town. I swear, you two just are not cool," said the first rider.

The camels drank their fill of the water. The riders mounted them. They rode on as the sun began to set, throwing long, silent shadows behind them. The camels walked with a steady, rhythmic pace. The riders swayed side to side with each long graceful stride of the camels. The wind creeped over the dunes, cooling as the sun set.

When they reached the town, the first rider said, "Hey, there's a little café over there. Let's go get some juice or something so we can clear the desert dust from our throats."

They rode over to the café and got off their camels. As they walked toward the doorway, the first rider stopped. "Like I said, I am too cool to be carrying rocks around in my pockets." He reached into his pocket, pulled out his hand. and discovered he had three pieces of gold!"

The second rider said, "What'd you get? Should I look at mine?" He stuck his hands in his pocket and found he had a hand full of gold!

The third rider reached both hands deep into his pockets. He pulled his hands out and began jumping around, gold spilling to the ground, "I'm rich! I'M RICH! I'M RICH!"

And, just as the voice said, each of them was happy, and each of them was sad. Why were they happy? Because they had listened some and picked up something. But they were sad.

Why? Because they didn't listen more and pick up more. And remember, there are no landmarks in the desert. The dunes are always shifting. They could never come through that same place again. So in all passages of life, especially during the educational years, listen all you can, pick up all you can, for you can never come through that same place again.

42

Dress Up Plain Truths and Facts (a folktale)

LARRY GRANT COLEMAN

A YOUNG DIVINITY STUDENT once asked her teacher and mentor, who was a bishop, a great preacher, and father in the ministry to dozens of young men and women, why he always told a story in order to help explain the wisdom and truth found in the Holy Bible. The preacher answered the young lady by saying, "My daughter, let me tell you a story about why I do that. . . . "

A long, long time ago, Naked Truth walked around on the earth traveling from town to town and from village to village trying to share his own great wisdom with the people who lived in those places. But, alas, because Truth was naked, nobody wanted to listen to him. "Get away from us, we cannot stand to look at you in that condition. Please leave us alone we cannot face you or deal with you in this Naked condition of yours." Naked Truth was almost shattered by this tragic experience of trying to share his wisdom and knowledge with people who could not stand the sight of him.

One day a wise woman came down from her mountain home to tell Truth about a beautiful palace and land ruled by a great and wise king! She told him that this wise king, whose name was Parable, could help Truth out of his terrible situation. Truth headed for the castle of this great king. He quickened his pace as he approached an incredibly beautiful edifice whose entering roads and footpaths were paved with jewels and gold. Parable's castle was surrounded by a river that shone like liquid silver. The music that came from the castle walls coaxed everyone there into a mood of joy and celebration.

Truth bowed humbly before the great king, who was also known by his nickname, "Storyteller." He told the king of his misfortune how everyone rejected him for simply wanting to share plain wisdom, knowledge, and truth. King Parable received Truth as if he were his own brother, and the king clapped his hands and said: "Servants, bring my friend here several of my finest robes and scarves, a drum, bells, some of my best jeweled musical caps, and six pair of golden musical, magical slippers." The king dressed Truth like he had never been dressed before and sent him merrily along his way. Now Truth began dancing and singing his way from town to town and village to village. And everywhere he went children and adults alike surrounded him so they could listen to what he had to say with great attention and focus. Truth was now dressed up in the clothes of Parable.

"That, my daughter," said the great master preacher, "is why I always share the great truths of the Holy Bible through the telling of stories."

NOTE:
There is power in "the story" because it appeals to people in a special way; it can be emotionally moving; it is entertaining. People can easily remember the story and all the learning points that are attached to the story, and because it touches people at their current level of development and helps to move them along.

Contributors

MUT NEFERIETH AMENICHI uses her talents to enlighten and educate her audiences and to preserve the storytelling tradition. She lectures about ancient Egyptian mythology and lives in the New York City area.

CHARLES AUSTIN is an occupational and environmental health scientist, multimedia designer, and an artist. He grew up in New York City and now lives with his wife and son in Upper Marlboro, Maryland.

MICHELLE AUSTIN is a high school student who will attend the College of Sequoias in northern California. She is chair of her high school's storytelling troupe and enjoys helping people realize the importance of storytelling.

YSAYE M. BARNWELL, PH.D., is a speech pathologist with a doctorate in cranio-facial studies. Since 1979 she has performed with the internationally acclaimed a cappella quintet, Sweet Honey In The Rock.

JANICE "JAWARA" BISHOP is an educator in Philadelphia, Pennsylvania. She is cofounder of Keepers of the Culture, Philadelphia's Afro-centric storytelling organization. Jawara, which means "peace loving," is married and the mother of four young adults and grandmother of nine.

BARBARA A. BURLEY is a contracting officer with the U.S. Department of Justice in Washington, D.C. She resides in Baltimore, Maryland, with her daughter Jessica and her mother.

AVERY H. COLEMAN is a retired Chicago Public School teacher. She resides in Chicago, Illinois, with her daughter and two of her grandchildren.

DEBORAH PEAKS COLEMAN is a public relations consultant and art dealer in the Baltimore, Maryland, and Washington, D.C., areas. A 1978 honor graduate of the Howard University School of Communications, she is publisher of the *Black Women in Ministry* calendar. She and her husband, Larry Grant Coleman, are members of Payne Memorial A.M.E. Church in Baltimore. Deborah can be reached at <www. potliquor.com>.

Larry Grant Coleman, Ph.D., has taught at the universities of Pittsburgh and Texas and at Morgan State, Howard, and Gallaudet Universities. Coleman is a member of the Omega Psi Phi Fraternity, Inc., the National Communication Association, and the National Training Laboratory (NTL) Institute. He is married to Deborah Peaks Coleman, and they reside in Baltimore, Maryland. Larry can be reached at <www.potliquor.com>.

Kevin Cordi is an educator who is chairperson of Youth Storytelling for the National Storytelling Network. He holds a master's degree in storytelling and education and is coauthor of a forthcoming book on storytelling troupes and groups.

Jack L. Daniel, Ph.D., is the vice provost and a professor of communication at the University of Pittsburgh in Pittsburgh, Pennsylvania. He is a scholar who continues to research and write about African American communication behavior.

James Counts Early is the director of Cultural Heritage Policy at the Smithsonian Institution Center for Folklife and Cultural Heritage, Washington, D.C. He and his wife, Miriam Stewart Early, live in Washington, D.C.

Cheryl Evans, Ph.D., is an assistant professor of teacher education at Bloomfield College in Bloomfield, New Jersey, where she instructs undergraduate and post-baccalaureate teachers-in-training.

Diane Ferlatte is an internationally renowned storyteller. With a large repertoire of multicultural, multiracial stories and songs, she has inspired audiences throughout the world. She resides in Oakland with her husband Tom, and they are the parents of two young adults.

Constance Garcia-Barrio is a freelance writer and storyteller who lives in Philadelphia with her family.

Crystal Grant is the pen name of an entrepreneur who resides in Southfield, Mississippi, with her husband.

Bill Grimmette is a writer, director, actor, master storyteller, and motivational speaker. He is the past president of the National Association of Black Storytellers. Other original stories of his include "The Legend of Mel and Nin" and "The Legend of the Golden Kinara."

Cyril G. Guerra Jr. is an associate minister at Hopewell Missionary Baptist Church in Pompano Beach, Florida. He volunteers for community service through his fraternity, Omega Psi Phi. He resides in Fort Lauderdale, Florida, with his wife, Joycine, and daughter, Ashley.

ELAINE ROBBINS HARRIS is an organization development consultant. She resides in Chicago with her husband.

HUGH MORGAN HILL (Brother Blue) is often referred to as "the world's greatest storyteller." He has taught storytelling in prisons, schools, colleges, and universities in the United States and abroad. He has received degrees from Harvard College and the Yale School of Drama.

ELEANOR HOOKS, PH.D., is a training and consulting specialist in diversity, leadership development, and organizational development. President and founder of Lifeskills International, she is author of *Some Folks . . . Somethin' to Say about Life*. She lives in Fayetteville, Georgia.

RUBYE H. HOWARD is a retired educator in the Atlanta Public Schools. An avid traveler, reader, and political and civic leader, she uses writing and photography to create personalized "one-of-a-kind" books for family and friends.

FREEMAN A. HRABOWSKI III, PH.D., has served as president of the University of Maryland at Baltimore County (UMBC) since May 1992. He is coauthor of the book, *Beating the Odds*, which addresses parenting and high-achieving African American men.

NORLISHIA A. JACKSON is senior writer and editor at Bennett College. Her articles have been published in *Essence*, *Purpose*, and other magazines. She resides in Camp Spring, Maryland, and has two daughters.

H. LOUISE LASSITER is a retired assistant principal of Walbrook Senior High School. She lives in Baltimore, Maryland, with her husband, Dr. E. Lee Lassiter.

DARLENE LEDOUX, PH.D., has dedicated over twenty-five years of service to children and families as an educator in Colorado. She is the past president of the Colorado Association of Elementary School Principals and is an advocate of bilingual education.

MIMI LEIBMAN, PH.D., has been active in the field of human relations since 1980. She has a Ph.D. in psychology and has been involved in teaching and research since 1963. Presently, she is a human relations facilitator for the Yonkers public schools.

ALYCE P. LITTLE is a retired State of North Carolina employee. She currently works part time with the Durham (North Carolina) Police Department. She describes herself as "single and happy." She is a long-time member of Mt. Vernon Baptist Church in Durham.

CHERYL "SPARKLE" MOSLEY is a storyteller, writer, speaker, and television producer-host. She is president-elect of the National Association of Black Storytellers and president of the North Carolina Black Storytellers Association. She resides in Charlotte, North Carolina.

Bobby Norfolk is a nationally recognized writer and storyteller. He and his wife, Sherry, are the authors of *The Moral of the Story Folktales for Character Development*.

Tejumola Ologbini is an internationally recognized storyteller and drummer who hails from Milwaukee, Wisconsin. His stories have appeared in several publications, including the book *Talk that Talk*, edited by Linda Goss and Marian Barnes.

Deidra K. Perry is the area manager for the Newspapers in Education (NIE) Program with *The Birmingham Times*. She is a past member of the national executive board for Delta Sigma Theta Sorority, Inc. Deidra is also a motivational speaker.

Joseph Petrella is currently serving as the project coordinator for the School-to-Work Initiative at Bronx Community College in the Bronx, New York. He was superintendent of schools (District 28, Queens) in the New York City School System.

Glennis Powell-Gill, a former teacher and administrator, works as a cluster leader for the National Center on Education and the Economy. She and her husband, Robert W. Gill Sr., live in Upper Marlboro, Maryland. They are the parents of three sons and one daughter.

Florence Roach is a teacher/administrator with Memphis (Tennessee) City Schools. She believes that teaching is a "calling." Flo is also a professional actress and singer.

Edward R. Robinson is an award-winning educator. He teaches math at DeWitt Clinton High School (Bronx, New York) and is the cochairperson of the Bronx-Westchester Scholarship Fund Program. Ed is married to Marguerite Twyne.

Ruth Travis is a retired physical education teacher with the Baltimore City Public Schools. She serves as the pastor of Evergreen African Methodist Episcopal Church. Rev. Travis lives in Owings Mills, Maryland.

Linda Vilches received a master's degree in education from Long Island University in 1993. She teaches in Yonkers, New York, and lives with her husband and daughter in Ossining, New York.

Deborah Wortham, Ed.D, is a twenty-eight-year education professional who has served as a teacher, principal, and administrator in the Baltimore City Public Schools. She resides in Ellicott City, Maryland, with her husband.